GARDEN STYLE
Decorating

By Cynthia Bix and the Editors of Sunset Books

SUNSET BOOKS ❧ MENLO PARK, CALIFORNIA

SUNSET BOOKS

Vice President, General Manager: Richard A. Smeby
Vice President, Editorial Director: Bob Doyle
Production Director: Lory Day
Art Director: Vasken Guiragossian

STAFF FOR THIS BOOK

Developmental Editor: Linda J. Selden
Copy Editor and Indexer: Pamela Evans
Design and Page Production: Nina Bookbinder
Photo Director/Stylist: JoAnn Masaoka Van Atta
Photo Researcher: Emily Abernathy-Jones
Production Coordinator: Patricia S. Williams
Proofreader: Mary Roybal

10 9 8 7 6 5 4 3
First printing January 2001
ISBN 0-376-01231-5
Library of Congress Catalog Card Number: 00-109154
Printed in the United States.
For additional copies of *Garden Style Decorating* or any other Sunset book, call 1-800-526-5111, or see our web site at www.sunsetbooks.com.

Cover: Abloom with dazzling color, lavish tabletop bouquets perfectly embody the sunny spirit of garden-style decorating. Designer: Rosmari Agostini. Stylist: Mary Jane Ryburn. Photographer: Barry Lewis. Cover designer: Vasken Guiragossian.

If you love gardens and long to bring their bright, fresh-air beauty into your home, this is the book for you. On these pages, you'll find a treasure trove of garden-style decorating ideas and inspiration—all beautifully illustrated with a wealth of photos—for transforming indoor rooms, sunrooms, and transitional areas like porches and verandas into rooms alive with the joys of the garden.

In preparing this book we were helped by many people who gave their time and expertise and also provided us with some of the beautiful garden decor elements we've pictured. Foremost among them are Martin Spector of GardenHome in St. Helena and Berkeley, California (with stylists Ginger Langford and Randi Herman); owner Alta Tingle, manager Linda Brauer, and Cindy Pugh of The Gardener in Berkeley and Healdsburg, California; and owner Diana Pullman of Pullman & Company in Mill Valley, California. We would like to acknowledge the Pasadena Showcase House of Design, The Napa Valley Designer's Showcase, and The San Francisco Decorator Showcase 2000. We are especially grateful to the homeowners who so generously allowed us to photograph their lovely garden rooms.

contents

in the garden spirit	4
garden room style	6
beautiful rooms	38
living inside out	82
elements of style	106
resources	140
index	144

special features

collector's corner	48
tablescapes	64
fabulous flowers	76
special effects	80
garden party	92
flowerspaces	100

IN THE GARDEN Spirit

think "garden room," and what do you imagine? Perhaps you visualize a glass-walled sunroom filled with houseplants and comfortable wicker chairs. Or you may think of an old-fashioned veranda, complete with porch swing and lemonade, or of a handsome contemporary living room where sunlight streams through French doors that usher visitors to a patio and garden beyond. Perhaps a looser interpretation occurs to you. Your vision may be an airy bedroom hung with breeze-blown curtains and alive with floral fabrics and cut flowers—or even a casual country kitchen sporting rows of herbs in pots on the windowsill and colorful vegetables, just brought in from the garden, heaped on a scrubbed wood table.

What all these images have in common is a unique spirit and style inspired by the life of the garden. That spirit is expressed in a love of growing things, of sunlight, of breezes and fragrances. Your garden room needn't be as elaborate as a glass sunroom or even a balcony or porch. Whenever you pull up a table and chair to a sunny window with a garden view, arrange greenery on a sideboard, or furnish a bedroom with fresh, flower-patterned linens, you are following an impulse to create a room that has the feel of a garden. Filling any room with garden touches creates an intangible bridge between indoors and outdoors. That's something you can do anywhere—in a city apartment or a country farmhouse—and in any climate, from Maine to Southern California.

A garden room can be any part of the house—a living room, dining area, bedroom, sunroom, or other room—or simply connected to it, as a porch, balcony, or breezeway. Sometimes, but not always, it may feature actual garden furniture and ornaments brought indoors. Most important, it's a room that celebrates the delights of nature—plants and flowers, sunshine and fresh air, and that wonderful feeling of relaxation and ease—that are always to be found out in the garden.

As you leaf through this book, you'll see in how many fresh and delightful ways the garden room idea can be interpreted. From sweeping views of dramatic rooms to charming decorative details—flowerpots, beautiful plates, and imaginative wall treatments—we show all the ways your love of gardens can be expressed in the spaces in which you live and work every day.

GARDEN ROOM
Style

The charms of garden room decoration lie in its ability to capture, indoors, the elusive pleasures of nature. It's as light as a sunlit meadow, as refreshing as a spring breeze, as colorful as a cottage garden in full bloom—all those fleeting delights that make gardens so appealing. Yet a garden room is there for you day after day, no matter what the weather or season. It's the perfect place to be indoors without losing sight of the garden's delights.

What makes it all succeed is a unique marriage of the arts of garden design and interior decorating. You borrow from the colors and textures of the outdoors to fashion rooms that celebrate nature and the seasons. By blending your own indoor and outdoor furnishings, ornaments, and plants, you create a truly unique garden room.

In the next few pages, you'll learn how interior garden style has evolved and what design elements make up the delightful versions that we enjoy today.

GARDEN ROOMS
the Inside Story

A GRAND TRADITION

That confection of glass and gingerbread adornments—the grand Victorian conservatory, or glasshouse—is the forerunner of today's garden rooms. During its golden age in England, especially, new technology enabled architects to construct marvelous structures using large, curved panes of glass held in place by thin frames of metal and wood. Adorned with domes and cupolas, the most famous of these grand greenhouse buildings included the Crystal Palace, built in London for the Great Exhibition of 1851, and the lovely Palm House at Kew Gardens. Those structures boasted state-of-the-art heating systems that made it possible to grow a veritable jungle of tropical plants year-round.

Domestic conservatories also became common in the grand manors of Great Britain and Europe, and eventually even in more modest middle-class homes. Although glasshouses began as showcases for exotic plant collections, later domestic conservatories (usually directly connected to the house) evolved into living spaces where Victorian families took afternoon tea and passed pleasant leisure hours. Furnished with wicker and wrought iron, lush with potted plants, and often softened with Oriental rugs, these rooms were relatively informal places in which to enjoy the delights of nature among the comforts of home. They were the first true garden rooms.

TOP: *Today, as in Victorian times, a garden room is a congenial setting for afternoon tea.*

CENTER: *Still a popular destination for garden lovers from all over the world, the Palm House at England's Kew Gardens features ornate ironwork beneath a soaring roof of glass.*

BOTTOM: *Fancy trim such as this is typical of the Victorian "gingerbread" style of decoration.*

OPPOSITE PAGE: *A contemporary interpretation of a Victorian design, this British glasshouse is a self-contained garden room.*

GARDEN ROOMS *the Inside Story*

ABOVE: *This contemporary interpretation of the garden room concept begins with a floor of limestone pavers. Natural materials are also featured in the bamboo furnishings and table base fashioned from a tree trunk. Potted tropical plants and an exotic, oversize floral arrangement further link the room with the garden outside.*

LEFT: *An antique botanical print, a tabletop ivy topiary, and a diminutive bird's nest—such casual collections of objects and motifs from nature on a tabletop or windowsill bring a touch of the outdoors into any room.*

RIGHT: *The fresh charm of a country garden brightens the dining area via a whimsical birdhouse piece on the wall, the natural texture of the woven chairs, and the bulbs and sunflowers on the antique pine table.*

CONTEMPORARY TRENDS

Today's conservatories are direct descendants of the Victorian concept. In modern homes, their cousins—solariums, or sunrooms—also feature glass walls and ceilings but are less often used as greenhouses; they're primarily intended as sunny, relaxing spaces for people. (Of course, they're also great places for plants, so long as temperature and moisture levels are controlled.)

These bright, airy spaces are the most obvious candidates for garden room decor. Large expanses of glass bring in views of the garden just beyond, as well as plenty of sunlight. A sunroom is the perfect place to furnish with real garden furniture, such as wire and wrought-iron chairs, stone-topped tables, and even garden ornaments like fountains, pedestals, and trellises. Furniture made of wicker, rattan, and other natural materials, brightened with colorful cushions and fabrics, is another clear choice for these fun, informal rooms.

Yet a sunroom is far from the only place in the home that benefits from garden room design. Any other room—from entryway to bedroom to kitchen—can also be decorated in garden style, using the same fresh, nature-inspired approach to color, pattern, and furnishings.

Garden room decoration is fun because its informality allows you to relax and indulge your most whimsical and creative notions. Why not hang your collection of vintage garden tools on a wall, or use a curlicue wrought-iron gate as a headboard for your bed? You have a golden opportunity here to create a fresh new style—perhaps using brighter colors, humorous touches, and loads of plants—for a room that may be quite different from the rest of the house. When you combine the arts of designing a garden and decorating a room, you're really free to choose from the best of both worlds.

A GARDEN
in Every Room

FRESH-AIR ROOMS

Which room will you choose in which to realize your garden fantasy? The most natural choice is a sunroom or enclosed porch . . . but any room that receives a healthy dose of light is a candidate. A windowed breakfast nook, a skylit kitchen, a living room with tall French doors opening onto a patio: all of these can be re-created in the image of the garden. Lacking these options, you can adapt the garden theme to enliven any room.

You can create a garden-inspired mini-office or studio simply by placing your desk or drawing table by a window, in a quiet corner where a screen of potted plants and the soothing sound of a miniature indoor fountain combine to make a perfect atmosphere for creative work. Or how about an informal gathering place for family and friends in an upper-story room that opens onto a tiny balcony? Comfortably furnished with wicker, perhaps with a trompe l'oeil garden scene painted on one wall and a borrowed view over the neighbors' treetops, it could reproduce the relaxing feeling of being in the garden. Even in a small bathroom, adding leafy plants and furnishings that suggest a porch or sunroom provides makeshift garden living.

TOP: *This nostalgic bathroom-cum-boudoir gains its effect from a Victorian-style wicker plant stand, a fern and flowers, and sheer draperies the color of sunshine.*

BOTTOM: *A miniature garden of freshly picked leaves and flowers blooms on a desktop. Along with some earthenware containers for office supplies, nature's gifts make working here a welcome task.*

OPPOSITE PAGE: *From the soft green paint to the fruit-and-leaf-motif wallpaper border and tapestry cushions, and from the bright, uncovered windows to the rattan-and-wicker chairs—every element of decor makes this sunny breakfast room feel like an extension of the garden just outside.*

A GARDEN *in Every Room*

HOW WILL YOUR GARDEN ROOM GROW?

The scale of your garden room project can be large or small. You may be starting from scratch, decorating or even building a new room from top to bottom—with custom-made windows, a dramatic raised ceiling, and brand-new flooring. If you're doing a complete redecorating job, you may be shopping for new furniture and accessories as well. In this case, you have no limits but your imagination (and, of course, your budget!).

On a more modest scale, perhaps you just want to give an existing room a lift. You might replace heavy old curtains with gauzy muslin swags, renew furniture with bright floral slipcovers, or bring in folding garden chairs freshened with a coat of white paint. You can fill the room with a collection of potted plants, frame pressed flowers for the wall, or stencil an old headboard with a leafy motif. Sometimes all it takes to convey garden style is a table set with garden-inspired dishes and linens, or a small wood ladder used as a plant stand. Touches like these—an investment of just a little time and imagination—will give tired rooms new life.

The particular combination of color and texture, plants and objects, is what makes each garden-style tableau individually yours. To re-create or interpret an outdoor scene that you treasure, choose from among its various elements and bring them indoors. On the following pages are examples that welcome in the garden spirit.

TOP: *This mantel display is simplicity itself, yet it evokes all the serenity of a quiet garden nook.*

CENTER: *Twining vines of ivy stenciled in pale green atop a chest of drawers call nature's beauties to mind. The leaf motif could be repeated throughout the room—for instance, in cushion fabrics or as a border under the crown molding or on the floor.*

BOTTOM: *Sunlight lends sparkle to an impromptu collection of bottles holding small offerings from the spring garden.*

OPPOSITE PAGE: *Garden ornaments are used in highly original ways in this rose-lover's bedroom: a wood trellis makes a display rack for a straw hat and floral-motif cards, a wire plant stand provides shelving, and painted buckets serve as magazine holders.*

ROOMS FOR ALL SEASONS

It's natural to visualize a garden room on a sunny summer day, with breezes blowing the curtains and golden light streaming in. Indeed, many garden rooms—especially transitional ones like porches, verandas, and some sunrooms—are strictly warm-season spaces. Yet conservatories originated as a way to create an indoor space for plants that would stay warm during cold winter months. And indeed, one of the greatest joys of any kind of garden room is being in a leafy, light place when everything outdoors is cold and gray. For avid gardeners, winter can be a frustrating season; but spending it in a garden room, tending indoor plants or sorting seed packets and browsing through catalogs, can make the season a restful interlude. For those who enjoy gardens less actively, the opportunity to be in a room that recalls the beauties of the growing season—sipping a cup of tea while gazing out at the snow-covered landscape or listening to rain on the roof—is one of life's great pleasures.

ABOVE: *On a winter's day, the sight of bright seed packets turns our thoughts to gardening. Sometimes the artwork on these small packets is handsome enough to be displayed in frames.*

TOP RIGHT: *Rain-washed windows look out on a gray scene, but a tabletop garden brightens the interior. The rose-covered tablecloth and cast-iron Victorian chairs enhance the theme.*

BOTTOM RIGHT: *Can spring be far behind? Fresh striped fabrics in sea breeze colors, white-painted wicker, and masses of florists' flowers carry occupants of this lovely room through the cold winter months.*

OPPOSITE PAGE: *Outside, snow blankets the ground. But inside, classic rattan furniture and potted palms convey the delightful impression of basking in tropical sunshine.*

A GARDEN *in Every Room*

BORROWED INSPIRATION

As you contemplate creating a garden room, look for inspiration to—where else?—the garden. Think of the colors and elements you love best in your own garden, or tour beautiful public gardens for ideas. Other good sources are garden shows, designer showcase homes, or even a walk around your own neighborhood. And, of course, tips abound in decorating and gardening books and magazines.

OPPOSITE PAGE: Just beyond the window, inspiration awaits. This stunning garden's intense palette of blues and pinks could inspire a complementary indoor room. The vibrantly hued roses, twinspur, clematis, and delphiniums might be echoed by paint, fabrics, and colorful glass or ceramic garden pieces.

RIGHT: *This garden might easily have been the model for the room decor shown below. A classic Victorian chair of white wicker and a lavish border of pink roses are elements that can be brought indoors, either as actual objects or as motifs.*

BELOW: *Reflecting the border of the garden shown at right, roses "bloom" indoors on fabrics and on the vintage rug underfoot.*

As you make use of these resources, notice what elements combine to attract you. White garden furniture set amid a profusion of flowering plants in pastel colors makes up one kind of scene. The intense yellows and reds of summer flowers surrounding rustic twig chairs or log benches convey a different impression. Formal gardens accented with shapely green topiary and snowy marble statuary bespeak a stately grace, whereas "found" objects artfully placed around the garden have shabby-chic appeal.

A favorite possession—an unusual garden chair, a lighthearted piece of garden statuary, or a handmade rag rug in soothingly faded colors—can inspire an entire room's design. Your painted Adirondack chair might become the linchpin for a room filled with the airy charm of a seaside summer cottage. That statuary may be your first piece in a collection of garden art that lends the whole room its character. And your old rag rug may be the centerpiece of an old-fashioned room filled with overstuffed furniture dressed in flowered cotton and an assemblage of vintage oil lamps. If you choose what you love, your garden room will be a place where you, your family, and your friends will always want to be.

THE COLORS
of Nature

THE GARDEN ROOM PALETTE

Choosing colors for your garden room is pure joy. Just as when planning a garden, you can follow your heart, selecting from the rainbow of colors those you especially love. But whether they're cheery Grandmother's-flower-garden hues such as cornflower blue and black-eyed-Susan gold, the delicate tints of a romantic rose bower, or the soothing greens of a shady woodland glen, garden room colors are all based firmly in nature.

Keep in mind that choosing color is one of the most emotional and subjective of decorating acts, and choosing color for garden rooms requires a special consciousness. What you're striving for is that elusive "I'll-know-it-when-I-see-it" quality of brightness and freshness found in the garden. It's an uplifting combination of color and light—the green of living things, the hues of blossoms, the soft tones of rock and earth, the ever-changing blues of the sky. In general, the colors you choose for garden rooms should be light, to reflect maximum natural and artificial light and to lend the room a fresh, open feeling. Shown on these pages are examples of palettes inspired by the many seasons and moods of the outdoors.

FRESH & LIGHT: *Reminiscent of a breezy spring day, rooms based on a fresh, light palette may feature soft shades of green paired with sunny yellow, white, or delicate pink. A room decorated in these colors looks as fresh as the outdoors; it makes you think of ferns, roses, and dainty lilies-of-the-valley. Combinations of white or cream with light taupe or other almost-neutral colors also convey a feeling of freshness and openness. And, of course, a room that features many subtle shades of white can look lightest and airiest of all.*

THE COLORS *of Nature*

BRIGHT & SUNNY: *The sizzling colors of summer are the ones you think of when you imagine a flower border blooming in the bright sunshine—the intense yellow and orange of marigolds and red-hot poker, the red of roses, the brilliant blue of delphiniums.*

A room decorated with bright, hot colors works best when you combine several intense colors that can stand up to one another, and when you use them as accents—in your choice of pillows on a chair, or in a collection of colorful glass vases, for example.

COLOR CUES

For inspiration, look outside. If there's a view of the garden from your windows, you might want to take your color cues from your plantings. You can also collect photos of other gardens and rooms you love, and clip examples from magazines. You'll soon notice a pattern to your choices—perhaps a preference for warm, earthy tones, or a consistent visual thrill when you view intense, zingy colors. As you begin to narrow down the shades you prefer, gather fabric swatches, paint chips—even flower cuttings—and use them to project how those colors will work together.

Don't forget that wood, wicker, and rattan furniture as well as flooring such as tile, brick, and stone have color, too. These elements and surfaces, either natural or painted, will be an important part of the mix, or palette, of colors in your garden room.

COLOR AND LIGHT

It's also vital to consider how the available light will affect the colors you choose. Natural light is an essential element in a garden, and ideally there's a lot of natural light streaming into your room. Rooms with a southern exposure get plenty of warm natural light; those with a northern exposure will have cooler, less direct light. Designers usually advise using color to visually balance the "temperature" of a room. Try using warm colors (in the red, orange, and yellow range) for north-facing rooms, cool ones (blues, greens, and violets) for south-facing ones. Of course, some rooms require artificial light even in the daytime, and all do by night. Be sure to check the way your proposed colors look in artificial light; they may surprise you!

With these basics in mind, look at the photos throughout this book for inspiring garden room palettes. Note how the colors of walls, fabrics, and accessories interact with one another and set the mood and tone of each room.

Then feel free to use all of these examples as springboards for creating your own personal mix.

WARM & EARTHY: These are the colors of the land—of sand, stone, wood, and natural fibers such as willow and seagrass. Although some of them are "neutral" colors, they have their own richness, especially in textured materials like rough wood, linen, canvas, or earthenware. Terra-cotta shades, ocher, and deeper greens can contribute warm tones to an earthy palette. The overall effect of a room featuring these colors is one that envelops and soothes the spirit.

PATTERNS
and Textures

PATTERNS FROM THE GARDEN

The myriad patterns of garden plants are surely one of nature's miracles. Flowers display an endless variety of patterns, from the sun-ray arrangement of daisy petals to the striking "faces" of pansies. It's no wonder that floral motifs are among the most enduring and delightful in the pantheon of print design. From the charming chintz mixtures of classic English rooms to the bold, brilliant patterns of tropical style, depictions of flowers have enlivened soft furnishings for centuries.

Another favorite motif—the leaf—is equally ubiquitous. Leaves are arranged in complex patterns along their stems, sport multitudinous shapes, and reveal intricate veining. In choosing fabrics, wallpapers, rugs, and even stencil patterns, you can replicate these natural motifs as well as more unusual ones: nature and wildlife designs featuring birds, bees, fruit and vegetables, or even detailed country-life scenes such as those on toile fabrics. These delightful patterns, so reminiscent of the garden, can be combined to pleasing effect with stripes, dots, checks, and plaids.

Remember that elements such as the grain in a wood floor or the woven strands of a seagrass mat are patterns, too—subtler, but another visual factor to consider in your overall mix.

RIGHT: *Three striking patterns from the plant world include the rows of spines covering the barrel cacti (top), the dramatic striped leaves of a variegated canna (center), and the speckled pouches of the pocketbook plant (bottom).*

OPPOSITE PAGE: *Mixing patterns of various sizes helps set the style of this light, cheery room. The settee's medium-scale leaf print is a perfect counterpoint to the fresh, larger-scale zinnia pattern of the chair, bench, and accent pillows. The delicate patterns of both indoor and outdoor plants contribute another layer of interest. Bold geometric floor tiles add "punch."*

PATTERNS *and Textures*

NATURE'S TEXTURES

Nature is replete with infinite tactile textures: the roughness of bark, the slickness of wet rock, the soft and velvety feel of moss. Plant texture varies, too: leaves and flowers may be glossy or matte surfaced, fuzzy or prickly, bumpy or smooth. In a garden room, echoes of textures from the garden similarly contribute to a room's special ambience. The most successful rooms reveal a skillful blend of those textures, just as in nature's happiest juxtapositions.

One way to echo the garden indoors is to incorporate elements common in nature. Wood, finished or rough-hewn, appears in floors and woodwork, furnishings, and ornamental objects. Vines and reeds (rattan, wicker, and caned furnishings and accessories) and grasses (sisal or seagrass rugs) can add layers of texture to living spaces. Stone (in floors, countertops, and sculpture) is a powerful natural element. Every geographical region has its particular kinds of stone, and each one—limestone, granite, bluestone, marble—its own distinctive texture, pattern, and color. And of course plants, both living and preserved, are the easiest of all natural elements to integrate into a room.

RIGHT: *Texture can be taken directly from nature in the materials you use to furnish a garden room. Bamboo, for example, has handsome stems with smooth surfaces and wonderfully knobby joints. Bamboo is beautiful whether green and growing or cut, dried, and bent or woven into striking patterns, as shown in the screen at top. The chair shown below it is made from a creative combination of split and whole bamboo.*

COMBINING PATTERN AND TEXTURE WITH COLOR

The interplay among texture, pattern, and color is what gives a room character and interest. Although mixing these elements skillfully may seem daunting, it's really not difficult if you follow a few simple guidelines.

First, remember that patterns vary in scale, from small ones (which "read" as solid or textured from a distance) to large ones (which are best used sparingly and with care). Medium-scale patterns are the most versatile, because their designs can be read even from a distance yet are seldom overwhelming. You can successfully combine patterns of different scales in one room if they share common colors; just don't vary them too widely. And for a pleasing visual rhythm, distribute patterns throughout your room rather than clustering them.

When choosing textures, don't forget how they influence our perception of color. Heavily textured materials such as canvas absorb rather than reflect light, so they make colors appear muted or more earthy. Smooth, shiny surfaces such as silk make colors appear brighter than they are. When combining textures, use a variety, just as you do with patterns. Set a rattan chair next to a glass-topped table, or place a rustic twig basket on a smooth, polished wood floor. When you're working with more than one color, you can use similar textures—a thick, braided rug and a twill-upholstered chair, for example—to unite them. As you leaf through this book, you'll find examples aplenty of how to use patterns and textures in garden rooms.

TOP: *The rough surface of a stone wall calls for fabrics and furnishings of equally strong texture. Pillows of leather and nubby woven wool fill the bill and carry out the rough-and-ready Western theme.*

BOTTOM: *This room has it all—the rough textures of woven grass matting and old wood against the smooth, shiny texture of pottery. The small-scale patterns of the matting, bamboo, and accent pillows are balanced by the larger-scale pattern on the sofa. All are united by the warm color palette.*

29

LIGHT-FILLED
Indoor Spaces

LETTING IN NATURAL LIGHT

Outdoors in the garden, fresh air and sunlight are primary sources of life, color, and growth. When you bring natural light and air into your garden room, you're bringing in the very essence of the outdoors.

Ideally, your prospective garden room has a generous number of windows. Of course, a glass-walled sunroom or solarium would be perfect; but most rooms have at least a couple of windows, and sometimes glazed doors leading outside as well. Even in a room whose windows are small or few, you may be able to add light through a strategically placed skylight.

Unless you're remodeling and adding new wall openings, however, the key to letting in light is to make the most of whatever you already have. Your task is easier if you have south-facing windows and doors, which let in brighter light than the softer, more diffuse light of north-facing ones. Where privacy is not an issue, you might leave windows uncovered. Or give them a light

and airy treatment, with casual swags of gauzy fabric, translucent shades, or flowing, unlined draperies in light colors and fabrics that let the sunlight stream through and the breezes flutter. (For fresh window treatment ideas, turn to pages 116-117, and see the other imaginative examples throughout this book.)

Another way to add natural light is to use mirrors and faceted glass objects like vases and sculptures. Positioned carefully—so that what they reflect is pleasing to the eye, yet the light they catch doesn't become a blinding glare—mirrors can do a remarkable job of brightening a room.

ABOVE: *Sunlight streaming through a nearby window makes working at this prettily appointed potting sink feel like being out in the garden on a warm spring morning. The fabric's soft greens and the wood's honey tones carry out the springtime theme.*

OPPOSITE PAGE, TOP: *Spiral glass candlesticks, ornaments with silver bases, and a tall mirror on the wall glitter when touched by sunshine. Light is further amplified by the table's gleaming, reflective surface.*

OPPOSITE PAGE, BOTTOM: *An overhanging trellis outside casts intriguing patterns of sunlight and shadow across this living room's floor and furnishings. A soaring ceiling, clerestory windows opening into the adjoining room, and light, neutral colors add to the open feeling.*

LIGHT-FILLED *Indoor Spaces*

CREATIVE LIGHTING

Lots of natural daylight is the ideal. But, of course, there are overcast days when you may need to give nature a boost with creative indoor lighting. And in any room you use at night, effective lighting can make the difference between a dull, uninviting space and a cozy retreat.

Often overlooked in lighting design is how daytime features seem to change when the sun is replaced by artificial light. Be sure that your carefully chosen window treatments look equally good at night; white curtains, for example, may look dingy in artificial light. And plan on mounting outdoor lights outside of uncovered windows; otherwise, they can look black and forbidding at night from within.

To get the most out of your garden room at night, you might combine several types of lights. Overhead lighting from different sources, evenly distributed around the room, creates soft ambient light. Recessed ceiling lights, cove and soffit lighting, and wall washers are all good fixtures for that effect. Uplighting a pale-colored ceiling can also evenly brighten your garden room by night. Incandescent bulbs give off a cheery golden glow; but for the brightest, purest white light, use halogen bulbs. These really turn up the wattage and can make a room as bright as day.

For extra drama, plan for strategically placed accent lights: tiny halogen fixtures to illuminate artwork, spotlights hidden among potted plants, and strip lights along book or display shelves. These add character as well as brightness. For a charming garden room touch, consider using outdoor porch- or patio-style fixtures such as lanterns, adapted for indoor use.

Finally, don't overlook the allure of natural nighttime light in the form of candles, oil lamps, and firelight. Candles can provide evocative fragrance as well as soft, lovely light, and the myriad designs and colors now available are decorative by day, too.

ABOVE: *A water-filled glass bowl of floating candles and flowers is easy to assemble and adds instant romance and color to the nighttime scene. You can coordinate the candle colors and blossoms with any room's palette.*

BELOW: *Backlighting a stately bamboo palm transforms it into a dramatic living sculpture by night. The glow from a trio of beeswax pillar candles, along with that of a nearby table lamp (not shown), makes this study an inviting evening retreat.*

OPPOSITE PAGE: *As the last of the day's natural light beams softly through skylight and French doors, this dramatic space comes alive with expertly designed nighttime lighting. Strategically placed track lights shine from on high, illuminating table, artwork, and the gleaming bronze sculpture. Traditional candelabra sconces add visual interest as well as a softer light that is echoed by the table's candles.*

WELL-APPOINTED
Garden Rooms

BEGUILING BASICS

In a garden room, every element, from the chair you sit on to the ceramic bowl you fill with spring flowers, has a special freshness. Although the basic elements are the same as for any room—wall and floor treatments; furniture; soft furnishings such as window coverings, upholstery, and cushions; and ornaments—those you choose for a garden room are distinguished by their connection with the outdoors. This means that the materials used are, as much as possible, natural: stone, wood, natural fibers, and earthenware or tile. In soft furnishings, patterns and motifs also reflect nature.

The furniture you choose for your garden room may be traditional in style and design yet still reflect the garden in its construction materials or upholstery fabric. An ordinary wood coffee table recalls the outdoors when painted pale green; a classic sofa shape looks fresh when upholstered in rose-printed chintz. Some indoor furniture's materials reflect the casual ease of outdoor entertaining—wicker and rattan, for instance. Your pieces may even have been intended for outdoor use. Teak benches and tables, folding wood-and-metal chairs, wrought-iron and wirework tables, canvas cushions, and even porch swings and hammocks can look wonderful indoors. All kinds of occasional pieces—plant étagères, side tables, and pedestals—can also be moved in from the patio to play supporting roles in your garden room.

TOP: *Laid in a strong geometric pattern, concrete tiles with a marbleized finish bring in the textures and hues of the outdoors.*

BOTTOM: *Simple matchstick blinds are an inexpensive, readily available option that adds natural texture and garden room style. Bamboo, grass, rattan, or reed blinds can be lined for privacy or embellished with trim for a variety of decorative effects.*

ABOVE: *Furnishing a room with pieces meant for outdoors creates instant garden ambience. This airy room looks and feels like an indoor patio thanks to the choice of flooring, furnishings, and accessories. From the metal bistro table and chairs to the wicker loveseat with its awning-striped pillows, from the tile floor to the wire plant holder on the wall, every element contributes to the sunny outdoor feeling.*

LEFT: *Cover a traditional sofa in a fresh, fern-print fabric, and—voilà!—the entire room takes on garden charm. Add plants, wicker, and filmy curtains, and you're all set.*

WELL-APPOINTED *Garden Rooms*

ABOVE: *A growing collection of birdhouses provided the inspiration for this imaginative display. A talented muralist created a "tree" for them to hang in: the branches were hand painted and the leaves were stamped onto them using shapes cut from dense foam. Three birdhouses hang from ceiling "branches" on fishing line; the others are furnished with eye hooks that allow them hang from cup hooks on the wall.*

LEFT: *A casual bouquet of hand-picked flowers adds a fresh, garden-style touch to any room.*

THOSE SPECIAL TOUCHES

Perhaps the most fun to bring indoors are true garden ornaments and utilitarian objects. From sundials to statuary, from fountains to watering cans, these practical yet visually pleasing pieces bring the charm and informality of the garden right into your home. An unadorned topiary frame set in a terra-cotta pot becomes an arresting tabletop sculpture; painted panels of false-perspective trelliswork turn a dining room wall into a three-dimensional garden space. As with all ornaments, such pieces can be new or of ancient pedigree, already weathered to a priceless patina.

Perhaps the single most effective and least costly decorative element is plants. A fragrant bouquet of cut flowers brings instant springtime to any room. A generous collection of growing plants in attractive containers can be massed to make an indoor garden; they quite literally freshen a room as they absorb carbon dioxide and return pure oxygen to the air. And for high style there's nothing so dramatic as an artful arrangement of dried flowers, stems, vines, or branches; they can take on the quality of sculpture when thoughtfully displayed.

These and other "extras" are really the heart and soul of your garden room, because they give it a flair and personality all its (and your) own. As you page through this book, you'll see many examples of garden-style furnishings, art, and accessories. On pages 124–129, especially, you'll find ideas and inspiration for choosing and using these elements in new and exciting ways. Adapt those ideas and make them your own!

ABOVE: *Avid collectors come up with all kinds of marvelous accessories from the outdoors, as this old goat cart demonstrates. Besides providing a resting place for pet chickens that occasionally wander indoors, the straw-filled cart makes a delightful addition to an eclectic corner tableau of baskets, dried and fresh flowers, and—yes—a chicken (but this one's not real).*

LEFT: *Vintage garden furniture and implements are a popular choice for decorating garden rooms.*

BEAUTIFUL
Rooms

There are as many ways to style a garden room as there are gardens. In this chapter, we offer various interpretations of garden style—in living rooms and sunrooms, kitchens and dining areas, bedrooms and baths. Many rooms have a special theme or "look" that's expressed in a host of creative details. From rooms that recall Grandma's country garden to spaces of Zen garden simplicity, from floral fantasies to sophisticated tropical hideaways, you'll see plenty of inspirational and imaginative styling.

No matter what the style, all of these rooms reflect an affinity for sunlight and fresh air and a delight in the endless variety of colors, patterns, and textures to be found in nature. Just as the gardener arranges and cultivates plants outdoors, so these garden lovers have designed indoor environments that sing with life, light, and color. So browse among these pages to glean ideas for your own beautiful room.

a summer-cottage charmer

OPPOSITE PAGE: *Architectural details such as the plate rail with its decorative molding and the beadboard wainscoting give this room the look of a turn-of-the-century cottage. French outdoor café furniture mingles with gracefully shaped pine settees for invitingly informal yet sophisticated comfort. The palette is soft, from the green paint on the wall panels to the prints chosen for the cushions, hooked rug, and handmade pillows. Mixing subtle stripes and plaids with the predominantly floral patterns adds more visual "punch."*

LEFT: *A garden-style corner by the window, furnished with bistro pieces and enhanced by garden urns overflowing with flowers and ivy, is an inviting place to sit and read or sip coffee.*

BELOW: *Glazed bifold doors open to let garden room and patio flow together. Using a continuous paving of Arizona flagstone indoors and out reinforces the connection, as does choosing the same style of furnishing for both sides of the glass.*

OPPOSITE PAGE: *Against a backdrop of clean lines and simple furnishings, a collection of folk-art pieces and flowers give this living room a fresh, country-garden feeling. Focusing on a few decorative "themes"—birdhouses, apples, and sunflowers—keeps this lighthearted look unified and uncluttered.*

ABOVE: *A tabletop garden-style display features bouquets in sizes from miniature to bold. Bright sunflowers burst from a watering can, surrounded by gaily colored bulbs and tubers.*

LEFT: *A picket-fence box bearing a harvest of apples recalls Grandmother's cottage; thematic companions are an old-fashioned garden whirligig and a wall display of tiny birdhouses.*

BELOW: *Arranging little vignettes with favorite objects makes decorating fun—and you can change them as often as you like, seasonally or just on a whim.*

in a country garden

BRIGHT FOLK-ART PIECES FROM THE
GARDEN BRING FRESH, LIVELY
STYLE TO A SIMPLE WHITE ROOM

OPPOSITE PAGE: *This light, bright room captures the sun's warmth and catches breezes through roof and side vents that open on balmy days. It's furnished in a simple, relaxing style with textured materials in neutral colors that relate to the world of nature visible just outside.*

RIGHT: *Stylish chairs and sofa boast wonderfully sculpted frames of ash and richly textured woven grass from the Philippines. The chenille-covered cushions and the seagrass matting underfoot add more of nature's textures.*

BELOW: *A montage of personal treasures can lend personality and depth to any room.*

windows on the sky

SIMPLICITY REIGNS
IN A LIGHT-BATHED
SPACE THAT SOOTHES
BOTH EYE AND SPIRIT

OPPOSITE PAGE: *The outdoors marches right into this bright garden room, with its assemblage of vintage furnishings that marry plants with objects from various periods and styles. The boundary between indoors and outdoors is blurred by the repetition of this eclectic style in the seating area just outside.*

TOP LEFT: *A wall-spanning trellis covers one side of the conservatory to support vines planted in large containers. They benefit from abundant light and a sunshine-hued backdrop.*

BOTTOM LEFT: *Outside, time-weathered Victorian wirework and wrought-iron furniture keep company with an assortment of plants in stone, terra-cotta, metal, and wood containers.*

BELOW: *The bust of a young lady provides a lovely, Victorian-style focal point in this garden-inspired tableau.*

relaxing in style

COMFORT AND STYLE BLEND
IN AN AIRY GARDEN RETREAT
JUST MADE FOR RELAXATION

Collecting pieces related to the garden is a passion that you can turn into a real decorating asset. Effective display is the key. If you have an extensive collection of baskets, for example, resist the urge to put them all out at once—it's better to focus on a few at a time and rotate them periodically. For maximum impact, group the items in your collection. A common theme—or aspects such as their shape, materials, and color—will be enough to unite them into a pleasing composition.

You can display small objects on a wall, along a shelf, on a table-top or windowsill. Large objects like urns or finials might go on the floor, where they will be appreciated but not stumbled over—flanking a fireplace, perhaps, or grouped in a corner by a patio door, or marching up a short flight of indoor steps.

COLLECTOR'S CORNER

OPPOSITE PAGE: *A light-hearted mixed-media grouping reflects one collector's love of barnyard critters. The bird's nest playfully suggests the chicken-and-the-egg dilemma!*

CLOCKWISE, *from upper left: In an imaginative twist on the fashion for decorated wreaths, a wall display features antique garden tools wired in place; an avian theme unites a tabletop assemblage that includes a bird's nest, old gravure prints of birds' eggs, and a single, perfect feather under glass; birdhouses of a feather flock together on a cleverly painted "tree"; color and function unite a collection of small glass vases scaled to fit a narrow decorative shelf; vintage finials of various shapes become decorative when clustered atop a table; and treasures collected from outdoors make a striking display and invite closer inspection when pressed into upright glass frames.*

49

a hearthside garden room

ABUNDANT NATURAL
LIGHT ILLUMINATES
A COZY GARDEN ROOM
CENTERED AROUND A
RUSTIC STONE HEARTH

OPPOSITE PAGE: *Warmth and sunlight stream through the glass roof of a family room made for relaxation. The roof and windows were constructed from a greenhouse kit and integrated into the basic structure of the room, which links the home's kitchen with the garage. The fireplace, of local stone, provides a focal point. The furnishings and ornaments— old and new wicker, an armillary-sphere sundial, potted plants—bring touches of the garden into this sunny space.*

ABOVE: *Grouping some "favorite things" between a matched pair of decorative objects like these small potted standards imposes a pleasing sense of order.*

RIGHT: *Roller shades made from solar-control screening are handy when the sun gets too intense.*

BELOW: *A random-laid slate floor acts as a passive solar collector, absorbing warmth during the day and radiating it back as the evening cools. For a soft, decorative touch, an area rug with a hint of garden leaves was laid atop the stone.*

a gallery of
flowers

A PAINTER'S LOVE OF
FLOWERS INSPIRES A
WORKING STUDIO BLOOMING
WITH CREATIVE ENERGY

OPPOSITE PAGE: *Everywhere you look in this painter's studio, details remind you of the garden. Of course, there are the artist's paintings themselves. But see what else you can spot—from a miniature gazebo to the floral-patterned floor cloths, garden-inspired artifacts and furnishings abound.*

ABOVE: *The paintings explore the endless variety of color, form, and pattern to be found among flowers. Here, a display of several of the artist's works surrounds a wicker table bearing a collection of mirrors framed by—what else?—flowers.*

old-world country style

PRIZED ARCHITECTURAL GARDEN FRAGMENTS EMBELLISH A LIVING SPACE AGLOW WITH THE COLORS OF THE EUROPEAN COUNTRYSIDE

OPPOSITE PAGE: *Ornamental objects left outdoors to weather acquire a patina that suggests their history and expresses their "soul." In this room, salvaged pieces include the doors themselves, the pediment above them (rescued from an old bank building), the tall stucco pedestal, and the stone finial serving as a doorstop.*

ABOVE: *The warm, approachable atmosphere of these rooms derives from vintage architectural pieces such as the urn (now a lamp) and the old iron brackets and hinges surrounding weathered shutter doors, as well as from the building materials themselves—salvaged column, beams, and lintels.*

TOP LEFT: *The owner-designer's personality is expressed in every detail. Here, a treasured painting of a local scene anchors a tabletop arrangement featuring soft lighting, plantings in an old French pottery bowl, and a collection of favorite glassware.*

BOTTOM LEFT: *Hovering over a doorway, a stone cherub (actually an antique fountain ornament) casts a benevolent eye over his domain.*

the gardener's kitchen

BRIGHT, SUNNY, GARDEN-INSPIRED
KITCHENS EVOKE THE BLITHE
SPIRIT OF OUTDOOR LIVING

ABOVE, TOP LEFT: *For a quick-and-easy garden touch in the kitchen, fill heatproof glasses with neatly arranged fresh vegetables in water; top each with a floating candle and enjoy them all as a countertop display.*

ABOVE, BOTTOM LEFT: *Produce stored in the kitchen can become part of your garden decor when kept in a garden-friendly container. Woven or wire baskets, decorative crates, trugs, and even terra-cotta pots are good candidates.*

ABOVE RIGHT: *Just a few hints suffice to convey the garden theme. Subtle statements in this kitchen include a softly textured natural burlap shade and a minigarden of potted herbs, some trained as miniature standards.*

RIGHT: *Flowering cabbage—part decorative, part edible—is an amusing choice for dressing up a kitchen counter.*

OPPOSITE PAGE: *An overall decorating scheme can transform an ordinary kitchen into a garden fantasy. Walls sponged in soft shades of verdigris and amber call up the image of a farm kitchen in the Tuscan countryside; weathered garden chairs and a European-style table reinforce the association. Even the watering can has a verdigris patina, as if it had done years of service in a kitchen garden.*

a sunny conservatory

A BREEZY URBAN ADD-ON OFFERS SUNSHINE AND FRESH AIR FOR PLANTS AND PEOPLE

OPPOSITE PAGE: *Just the right size for an intimate meal or a relaxing hour in the sunshine, this charming little conservatory room was built onto the back of the house using prefabricated components. An exterior staircase links the home directly with the backyard and psychologically extends the room. Each carefully thought-out detail within, from the small-scale upholstered chairs to the latticework shelf and narrow wicker planter, makes the most of the space and offers made-to-scale comfort and style.*

ABOVE: *Cotton table linens with a cheery floral design enliven the room and coordinate with the upholstery, creating an effective mix of pattern scale and color.*

RIGHT: *This tiny space expands, visually and literally, when the curtains are pulled back and the windows and doors are opened wide. The leafy vista makes a beautiful backdrop that finds its echo in the indoor plants—orchids and begonias—growing on the windowsill and in the potted plants on the staircase landing.*

RIGHT: *A wealth of artfully coordinated details makes this lovely all-season room a unique expression of its creators' vision. A venerable ficus rambles around the upper reaches of the room, sheltering a treasured collection of furnishings and trim materials. Resting on antique French pavers is a one-of-a-kind settee of wicker and metal, decoratively punched and hand painted. Behind it, adding an elegant architectural element to the bank of windows, a white-painted cast-iron railing is underscored by a border of Italian glazed ceramic tiles.*

ABOVE: *Vintage cast-iron furniture coordinates to perfection with the surrounding railings; the scene is reminiscent of an elegant Victorian conservatory.*

BELOW: *An antique glass-paned window salvaged from an old greenhouse is the crowning glory of the room; positioned over the window wall, it makes a fitting focal point.*

open-air elegance

dining in garden style

IMAGINATIVE ARRANGEMENTS OF PLANTS AND ORNAMENTS BRING ALL THE CHARMS OF THE GARDEN TO THE DINING TABLE

ABOVE LEFT: *This exuberant dining room overflows with lighthearted references to the garden, from the metal vines twining up walls and around windows to the table base's ornate leaf design in relief.*

ABOVE RIGHT: *Textural contrast is always intriguing; a case in point is the juxtaposition of this glittery, glass-and-metal piece with the organic shapes of fresh apples.*

RIGHT: *A large bowl of perfect oranges complements this sleek, minimalist dining area. The table itself, with its patio-style glass top and garlanded stone pedestal, makes a subtle reference to outdoor living.*

OPPOSITE PAGE: *Plants and accessories bring garden room magic to this bright dining area. An original, flower-bordered painting exudes folk-art charm, and fresh flowers from the owner's garden mix charmingly with foliage plants.*

Using your tabletop as a canvas, you can create a colorful "landscape" with garden-inspired tableware and accessories.

A centerpiece of dried or fresh-cut flowers is a classic. Or try twining fresh ivy cuttings or a floral garland along the tabletop. Small nursery plants—including grasses and mosses—can be tucked into a garden-themed container; hide their pots with a layer of sphagnum or Spanish moss. If space is limited, simply tuck sprigs of flowers and foliage into napkin rings at each setting.

Underlay your arrangements with linens and dishes in fresh colors; use designs such as flowers, leaves, or vegetables...even bugs!

And don't overlook the ambience that candlelight adds. To suit the theme, display candles in small outdoor lanterns.

TABLESCAPES

CLOCKWISE, *from top center: A centerpiece of vegetables and fruits creates a novel display whose earthy colors are repeated in the jaunty striped candles, tableware, and linens (note the playful details such as frog and dragonfly napkin rings); a bowl of freshly pureed soup gets the garden touch with an edible garnish of nasturtium flowers; gathered around a centerpiece of foliage and hydrangeas, place-setting bouquets are cleverly contained in scooped-out artichoke "vases"; candles for a harvest table are created from small winter squashes hollowed out to accommodate miniature votives; plates edged with a rustic basket-weave texture, leaf-scattered place mats, and colored glassware combine with a jug of sunflowers to make a tablescape worthy of van Gogh; and place mats of woven fiber paired with napkins featuring palm tree and leaf motifs convey a casual, tropical style perfect for patio or poolside dining.*

dreaming of the garden

BEDROOMS GRACED WITH THE CHARMS OF
FLORAL LINENS, FLOWERS, AND GARDEN
ORNAMENTS PROMISE SWEET DREAMS

OPPOSITE PAGE: *With its antique-style bed, light pastel color scheme, and garden-style accessories, this sweet bedroom brings to mind images of an old-fashioned cottage flower garden.*

LEFT: *An iron bed frame fashioned to resemble garden gates encloses a space in which to pass many restful hours.*

BELOW LEFT: *Hand-painted silk is the ultimate luxury in bed linens; here a fantasy orange grove flowers across the duvet, which tops a silk bedskirt in a complementary shade. Beyond the bed, glimpsed through sheer draperies, is a tiny private patio.*

BELOW RIGHT: *Silk velvet pillows hand painted in gold add softness and sheen, as well as a decorative accent, to the bedroom scene.*

RIGHT: *You can almost hear the whisper of a sea breeze rustling palm trees in the relaxed elegance of this inviting room. Every detail works to convey a sunny atmosphere redolent of lanai living. A palette of celadon and ocher, classic rattan furniture, and the repeated palm motif give the room a polished, pulled-together look, yet keep the spirit light.*

ABOVE: *Layered over bamboo blinds, cotton draperies in a refreshing tropical fruit-and-plant motif are banded in polished linen to match the sofa's upholstery. The curtain rods even have pineapple finials!*

FAR RIGHT, TOP: *Set into a limestone floor the color of beach sand is a handsome "rug" of stone mosaic.*

FAR RIGHT, BOTTOM: *Pillows, prints, fabrics, and accessories all coordinate in perfect harmony.*

lanai living

SUNNY COLORS, A PALM MOTIF, AND RATTAN FURNISHINGS EVOKE TROPICAL ISLAND STYLE WITH A TOUCH OF ELEGANCE

fresh-air bathing

FRESH AIR, LIGHT, AND DECORATIVE TOUCHES
FROM THE GARDEN GIVE BATHROOMS
A BRIGHT AND OPEN ATMOSPHERE

ABOVE LEFT: *New uses for ordinary flower lovers' accessories can be found even in the bathroom. Here, a hairpin-style flower holder makes a handy home for toothbrushes.*

ABOVE RIGHT: *Where privacy is assured, a bathroom that opens directly onto a deck and the landscape beyond can invite the garden indoors. The simplicity of natural-finish wood and polished granite gives this bathroom a Zen-like calm, in which the bather can appreciate the fresh air and leafy surroundings to the fullest.*

RIGHT: *An antique French garden basket finds another life as a bathroom towel holder. Below it, a weathered table displays fresh flowers—a simple but often overlooked way to beautify a bathroom.*

OPPOSITE PAGE: *A larger-than-life garden blooms and twines around the walls of an elegantly appointed bathroom. This spectacular wall treatment was created by painting with acrylics on canvas and then gluing the canvas to the walls like wallpaper.*

OPPOSITE PAGE: *This clean, very contemporary interpretation of the garden room idea begins with smooth, organic wood floor and furniture surfaces. These become the canvas against which to display an ever-evolving collection of dishes and bowls that hold small, finely focused "dish gardens."*

TOP RIGHT: *A sculptural chest handcrafted of maple holds a stair-step display of planted white ceramic pots.*

BOTTOM RIGHT: *A sleek ceramic bowl contains a Lilliputian water garden of duckweed and watercress.*

BELOW, TOP: *Note the simple but arresting tabletop vignettes: three Japanese dishes in which float tiny leaves, and a square of textured glass laid over two perfect magnolia leaves. The simplicity of each composition invites the beholder to focus closely on each leaf and stem—to examine often overlooked details of nature as if they were tiny individual jewels.*

BELOW, BOTTOM: *A composition based on texture and light features clear glass vases atop a smooth stone surface, contrasted with a dark ceramic sake server.*

space and serenity

NATURE'S SMALL TREASURES
INHABIT A HYPNOTIC SPACE
LIKE MINIATURE ISLANDS
IN A TRANQUIL SEA

OPPOSITE PAGE: *Borrowing a garden view and profiting from soft natural light through dramatic floor-to-ceiling windows, this dining area makes use of a few large-scale pieces and striking architectural elements—like the ornate columns— to convey serene elegance. Against walls glazed in hues and textures suggesting antique silks, oversize ceramic pots support tall New Zealand laurels.*

ABOVE LEFT: *A tucked-away corner is transformed into a garden by a cluster of tropical plants in attractive pots.*

ABOVE RIGHT: *A Chinese-red furniture panel, delicately sketched with a garden scene, adds color and charm to the room.*

LEFT: *The plants chosen for this indoor garden tableau—including a tall bamboo stem and an oncidium orchid—combine to suggest the exotic allure of the Far East. The multicolored slate floor adds to the feeling of being outdoors.*

east meets west

ASIAN TRADITION SETS THE
STYLE FOR A SOFTLY LIT
CONTEMPORARY GARDEN ROOM

no one element brings the garden indoors the way floral bouquets do; their hues and scents give any room a lift. As you select flowers, keep your room in mind. Walls, furniture, or a favorite painting can inspire your bouquet's colors and style. For example, match a loose spray of mixed-color wildflowers with shabby-chic decor, but pristine white roses with a lacy boudoir.

Also consider the style and color of your containers; it's a creative challenge to match them to bouquets. And don't neglect other ways to display flowers. Garlands can be draped over mirrors, nosegays can define table settings, and cuttings can bloom at eye level in wall-hung containers. Although these effects will not be long-lasting, they have a special fleeting charm.

FABULOUS FLOWERS

THE MOST BEAUTIFUL FLOWERS

OPPOSITE PAGE, CLOCKWISE *from top left: Grouping glass vases of dark cuttings against a white wall takes advantage of shape and shadow; a unique jointed flower holder contains a meandering display of individual calla blooms for an eye-catching table topper; and a little deception—an everlasting garland of dried foliage and silk flora—makes a big impression when it frames a doorway to the deck.*

THIS PAGE, CLOCKWISE *from top left: An outdoor urn's luscious bouquet of hydrangeas, garden roses, sedum, and purple sage benefits from a hidden "bowl" of water (quickly made from a piece of double-ply plastic stapled together around the top); a galvanized metal flower-market bucket makes the ideal container for a loose, casual bouquet; a wall-hung steel cone holder bearing artichoke blossoms makes a striking display at eye level; and a single, perfect stem of a dramatic flower like this allium deserves to command the spotlight.*

RIGHT: *Plants are the stars of the show in this contemporary conservatory. The owners' spectacular collection of palms creates a tropical paradise against a backdrop of natural stone and glass.*

BELOW, TOP: *In such a room rattan chairs, with their open geometric patterns and cool cane seats, are the perfect choice.*

BELOW, BOTTOM: *Water cascades in a gleaming sheet down the smooth slate walls of the spa, like a waterfall splashing into a jungle pond.*

under tropical palms

IN A PALM-SHADED PARADISE,
EXOTIC FLOWERS BLOOM BESIDE
A GENTLY SPLASHING WATERFALL

SPECIAL EFFECTS

even if you lack a real garden, you can create the illusion of one with custom paint effects, whether intentionally two-dimensional or in the faux-painting style called trompe l'oeil (literally, "trick the eye"). Using shadowing and perspective, trompe l'oeil gives the illusion of three dimensions and can even conjure an entire garden scene, visible through a wall's "window." It is often cleverly mixed with actual objects—a vase of flowers painted above a real shelf, for example.

Besides providing a unique garden touch, specialty wall painting is a great problem solver. For instance, it can disguise an unpleasant structure such as a cinderblock wall or draw the eye away from an unattractive view.

Painters who achieve these remarkable effects can be found through interior decorators and paint stores. Ask to see the artist's portfolio or, if possible, on-site work.

OPPOSITE PAGE: *The elegant art form of another era finds fresh, contemporary expression in the painted ceiling and wall panels of this lofty curved dining room.*

CLOCKWISE, *from top left: A classical "vista," complete with faux stone window frame (painted above real shelves displaying kitchen treasures), brings the Italian countryside into a small pantry; a combination of folk-art objects and trompe l'oeil brightens a small corner; you can almost smell the lavender in this illusory Provençal field, skillfully depicted within a rustic stone arch set into a patio wall; and two mischievous cats, a rooster, and potted morning glories bring flora and fauna indoors to disguise a real-life dumbwaiter.*

LIVING
Inside Out

Living spaces bridging indoors and outdoors are particularly delightful to garden lovers. These transitional rooms let us enjoy fresh air and sunshine, as well as views of the garden and beyond, from partial shelter that provides indoor comforts.

This long-standing architectural tradition has taken many forms: old-fashioned front porches, graceful verandas, sunrooms, and many variations of enclosed patios. Decorating such indoor-outdoor rooms is just plain fun, whether you choose classics like wicker chairs, porch swings, and gliders or find new, whimsical uses for actual garden ornaments and accessories. Incorporating lavish floral upholstery fabrics, traditional draperies or blinds, and other typically indoor elements helps blend the room with the rest of the house.

Turn the page for a sampling of both traditional and unusual ways to decorate and live in these wonderful spaces.

southern hospitality

BEAUTIFULLY APPOINTED VERANDAS
EXTEND A GRACIOUS SOUTHERN-STYLE
WELCOME ON SUMMER AFTERNOONS

ABOVE: *An effective mix of traditional and contemporary styles in furnishings and architectural details characterizes this sheltered poolside gallery. It's well equipped for serving and enjoying alfresco meals by day or later, in the cool of the evening.*

LEFT: *Classical-inspired statuary adds just the right accent to this elegant formal veranda.*

FAR LEFT: *This quintessential Southern-style veranda is a graceful white-columned expanse overlooking a warm-weather landscape. Furnished to perfection with white wicker seating and glass-top tables, it's just the spot for enjoying a frosty drink. In a long, narrow space like this, there's room to create several seating areas: some for lounging, others for dining or playing games.*

BELOW: *Gauzy panels of nearly transparent nylon become magical veils of illusion that transform a poolside cabana into a serene retreat. The panels are anchored top and bottom to the posts, so that they move in the breeze yet remain relatively stable. Sunlight falls on a grouping of pillows covered in a French linen that's washable and surprisingly tough. Woven-grass mats on the floor conjure up images of a Japanese teahouse or temple. The container-grown weeping mulberry is a dramatic sculptural shape against the white shingled wall.*

OPPOSITE PAGE, TOP: *On a narrow shelf made from a salvaged piece of rough wood, orchids become a living work of art when aligned in simple wood cube planters.*

OPPOSITE PAGE, CENTER: *An antique Japanese stone container holds an offering of water hyacinths in bloom.*

OPPOSITE PAGE, BOTTOM: *The graceful shape of a low, modernist rocker belies its construction material—concrete. The chair's structure makes an elegant counterpoint to the softness of the pillows in this ethereal space.*

sun-dappled space

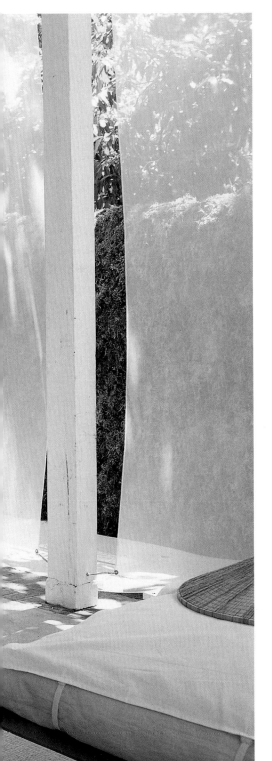

OPEN TO THE BREEZES, A CABANA
APPOINTED WITH THE UTMOST SIMPLICITY
INVITES SERENITY AND PEACE OF MIND

ABOVE: *The columned veranda over-looking a lush, sun-dappled garden has a faintly Moorish feel, the wicker furniture is Victorian, and the flowered and layered upholstery clearly declares "romance." The charm of this setting lies in the exuberant mixing of many elements—fabrics, furnishings, flowers, and accessories such as the large blue ceramic jars— successfully united by a soft pastel palette. Note how the richly layered fabrics and the elaborate chaise give this transitional space the feel of an indoor room.*

LEFT: *One detail within the larger picture is an eclectic assortment of jugs, vases, and vintage tin atop a weathered cabinet; the scene is artfully composed and unified by its soft, subtle blues and greens.*

a fantasy veranda

RICH HUES AND TEXTURES CREATE
AN ATMOSPHERE OF EXOTIC
ROMANCE ON A SUNNY VERANDA

LEFT: *What on earth is more romantic than roses? This bouquet appears especially lavish against a sunlit garden backdrop, among a collection of elegant vases and china pieces on a marble-top table. Grouping vases or other containers—some empty, some filled with flowers—makes an effective garden-style statement in any room, indoors or out.*

MARY EMMERLING'S
AMERICAN COUNTRY **COTTAGES**

Early American Herb Recipes

GREAT GARDENS

THE VICTORY GARDEN LANDSCAPE

tulip porch

WITH ITS BUILT-IN GARDEN MOTIF, AN OLD-FASHIONED PORCH DELIGHTS THE EYE AND WELCOMES VISITORS

ABOVE: *On this classic front porch, furniture and accessories carry out the old-timey theme. Painting the porch floor helped set off the cheery colors of the wood chairs—flea-market finds, all. On one chair rests Grandma's handmade quilt; appropriately enough, its design is the time-honored "Grandmother's Flower Garden."*

OPPOSITE PAGE, TOP LEFT: *The owner-designer got the inspiration for this charming cutout tulip motif from an old shutter glimpsed at a garden decorating shop.*

OPPOSITE PAGE, TOP RIGHT: *A collection of weathered wood finials makes an appropriate focal point on this porch; the paint on one piece just happened to match that on one of the chairs.*

OPPOSITE PAGE, BOTTOM: *Lattice below, fish-scale shingles above, and decorative molding in between combine to give this turn-of-the-century facade authentic period charm. Container-grown topiaries and standards marching up the steps add just the right touch and echo the stylized tulips-in-pots cutouts.*

C elebrate high summer with a colorful party buffet featuring bounty from the vegetable garden and the tools and containers you use to grow it.

Here, the buffet is served out on the porch. But on a chilly or rainy day, it could easily be set up indoors; in fact, staging a light-hearted party like this one could be just the thing to brighten up a dull day. You might seat guests in small groups around the house, at garden bistro tables dressed up with cheerful bouquets. Place cards might be fashioned from plant markers, and small herb-planted pots would make great party favors.

The examples pictured here show what fun you can have with the garden room idea when you begin to dream up fresh uses for your garden tools, accessories, and furnishings.

GARDEN PARTY

OPPOSITE PAGE: *When guests assemble on the porch, they'll be delighted by this colorful still-life composition—a buffet spread across a potting bench, served up in a variety of garden-themed containers.*

CLOCKWISE, *from upper left: A wire plant stand offers clean, paper-lined terra-cotta flowerpots full of munchies; iced drinks rest in a brand-new child's wheelbarrow; a glass garden cloche protects a selection of cheeses placed in a new garden sieve; buffet "plates" are new terra-cotta pot saucers lined with parchment paper (the decorative edges are cut with pinking shears); jelly jars make great drinking glasses, especially when provided with name tags cleverly fashioned from garden markers clipped onto twine; and a bright enameled watering can makes a useful pitcher.*

93

ABOVE: *A windowed porch makes a cozy retreat as afternoon wanes. Here, a rustic bench serves as a coffee table for an imaginatively cushioned wicker settee scattered with a highly individual selection of pillows.*

TOP LEFT: *Serene on an overcast day, this screened porch is a symphony of soft, neutral colors—in the cushions, the natural wicker, and even the wood decking.*

BOTTOM LEFT: *On a traditional open porch, simple matchstick blinds afford shade and privacy but can be raised easily to admit breezes and open up the space.*

OPPOSITE PAGE: *A screened porch is the practical choice in areas where summer brings biting insects. This old-fashioned charmer's screen "walls" overlook a leafy vista beyond, comfortably viewed from its collection of wicker rockers.*

private screening

PORCHES, SCREENED OR WINDOWED,
OFFER FRONT-ROW GARDEN VIEWS
AMID INTIMATE SURROUNDINGS

the best of both worlds

THOUGHTFULLY FURNISHED SPACES BRIDGE INDOORS
AND OUTDOORS, PROVIDING THE PLEASURES OF BOTH

ABOVE: *In this turn-of-the-century home, the porch is solidly backed by a wall of chunky granite; the garden comes up to meet it in the abundant plantings all around. The width of the porch allows ample seating on furniture that's well suited to the style of the house.*

LEFT: *The beauty of the craggy desert landscape in the background and the closer cultivated desert garden just beyond the house form a dramatic fourth "wall" for this stylish outdoor room. Bold, cast-cement furnishings echo the rocky terrain.*

OPPOSITE PAGE: *A room with two or three open-air sides offers indoor comforts along with the feeling of being at one with the surrounding landscape. The outdoor living room of this hilltop house combines a spectacular view with a cozy hearth and oversize, comfy woven-reed furniture.*

NEAR LEFT: *Indoor and outdoor rooms flow together almost seamlessly, united by a warm palette of wood tones and soft neutrals and by the beautiful fossilized flagstone floor, which runs throughout both spaces. The style and composition of the indoor furnishings—rattan with plump off-white cushions—also mirror those of their outdoor counterparts. A generous use of flowering plants makes the entire scene look like a garden.*

FAR LEFT, TOP: *Beneath the shelter of an architectural overhead blooming with jasmine, a seating area is lit by discreet downlights that make it a fully usable outdoor room by night. Strip lights along the horizontal beams add sparkle.*

FAR LEFT, BOTTOM: *Two sets of multifold glass-paned doors open the side and end of the room to the jasmine-wreathed patio.*

night and day

A DRAMATIC SPACE, BRIGHT AND OPEN BY DAY AND AGLOW BY NIGHT, IS THE ULTIMATE INDOOR-OUTDOOR ROOM

gathering an armful of fragrant sweet peas or tall-stemmed Peruvian lilies from the garden to arrange indoors is a time-honored way to beautify and freshen the home. Fortunate is the flower lover with a special nook in which to prepare and arrange these treasures.

This kind of garden room space can be both lovely and practical. You'll need a water source (preferably over a deep sink), a substantial work surface, and storage for containers, clippers, florists' foam, and other supplies.

To adorn your space, you might surround the sink with a floral fabric skirt to hide shelving below it. A nearby window can be curtained to match or left uncovered to a garden view. A shelftop collection of favorite containers can be a decorative element in itself. Extras might include paintings, a bulletin board display of inspirational bouquet ideas clipped from magazines, or an interesting outdoor light fixture.

FLOWER SPACES

OPPOSITE PAGE: *A flower arranger's little corner of the world is naturally pretty because of the blooms that adorn it; this particular spot gains extra character with the addition of utilitarian objects that suggest a bygone era. A commercial seed-packet display box rests on the pine worktable; a gardener's straw hat and apron hang from a wall hook.*

CLOCKWISE *from top: A deep double sink is ideal for conditioning flowers prior to arrangement and for cutting stems under water; in a generous space, a comfy garden-style chair for removing boots or studying catalogs is always welcome; a countertop that's attractive yet rugged enough to withstand scraping and the occasional jab with clippers or scissors is your best bet; and an assortment of "frogs"—one of the flower arranger's most useful tools—should be kept handy along with other supplies.*

101

a secret garden retreat

JUST STEPS FROM THE HOUSE, A SELF-CONTAINED
ROOM OFFERS RELAXATION AMID FURNISHINGS AND
ORNAMENTS BROUGHT STRAIGHT FROM THE GARDEN

OPPOSITE PAGE: *Beneath the handsome curved-beam ceiling of this garden house is an inviting space open to cooling breezes that bring the scents of the garden through open casement windows. The interior is furnished with a creative blend of the old and the new—an antique pine armoire holds a revolving display of favorite objects, while new garden chairs with a distressed finish offer comfortable seating. Note the delightful honeybee pillow!*

ABOVE: *Flowers gathered from the garden fill galvanized buckets, one of which is an old ice-cream container. A rugged floor of Connecticut bluestone tolerates plenty of foot traffic from outdoors, no matter how wet or muddy.*

LEFT: *The garden room's bell-shaped roof is fashioned of copper and recalls the classic designs of old European garden structures.*

OPPOSITE PAGE, TOP: *Against a background of painted hills seen over a crumbling "wall," a rustic bench beckons. In this inviting spot tucked beneath the eaves, star jasmine twines in company with dried vines. Toile curtains and pillows covered in assorted French-country-style fabrics contribute to the European ambience.*

OPPOSITE PAGE, BOTTOM: *The gentle splash of water provides a soft musical background to this enchanting scene; handmade tiles set into the stucco wall are in keeping with the patio's style.*

LEFT: *Shade cast by a wide market umbrella is welcome on a warm day in this intimate courtyard dining space. The weathered garden furniture has an old-world look that's been freshened with toile cushions and table coverings featuring floral motifs in varied scales.*

BELOW: *The kitchen connection with patio and courtyard is more than physical; European country style reigns here, as well. The garlanded hutch designed by the homeowner is the room's focal point. Many details, from the mantelpiece decor to the pictures on the wall, carry out the continental garden theme.*

patio pleasures

JUST PAST THE KITCHEN
DOOR, A COZY, VINE-WREATHED
SPACE OFFERS EUROPEAN-
STYLE ALFRESCO LIVING

Elements of style

Although any beautiful garden room is more than the sum of its parts, the individual ingredients that comprise it are what make it unique. Basic elements such as wall, floor, and window treatments set the stage. Paint the walls sunshine yellow or spread a sea grass mat beneath your feet, and you begin to get that outdoor feeling. Up go the curtains—perhaps panels of flowered sheer—and in come furnishings that recall the patio or porch. Finally, you add decorative pieces that convey your personal taste—an old stone trough, a pretty watering can, and, of course, plants.

Part of the trick to decorating a room in garden style is an ability to reenvision how things meant for outdoors might be used in an indoor setting. This chapter's pictorial idea gallery offers more than enough exciting garden room elements to set your own creative imagination working!

ON THE SURFACE

BOLD OR SUBTLE, CLASSIC OR QUIRKY, IMAGINATIVE WALL AND FLOOR TREATMENTS SET THE TONE OF A GARDEN ROOM. THEY MAY BE SUBTLE BACKDROPS OR MAY BECOME CONVERSATION PIECES IN THEIR OWN RIGHT, ESPECIALLY WHEN THEY FOOL THE EYE OR USE MATERIALS AND PATTERNS IN UNEXPECTED WAYS.

The photos on this page show how an imaginative use of tile, stone, and wood, as well as tricks with paint, can give indoor floors an outdoor look.

TOP, *left to right: Recalling a Mediterranean patio, hand-painted tiles grace interior stair risers; an intriguing "collage" underfoot features terra-cotta tiles, cement, and hardwood flooring in juxtaposition; and tiles of slate, dressed up with limestone strips and tiny glass mosaics, bring nature's textures and materials indoors.*

CENTER, *left to right: Stylized floral and vine motifs borrowed from Oriental rugs enliven an "area rug" created from floor tiles; a colorful crazy-quilt of tiles is mixed with pebbles and scattered with concrete "footprints" for a most creative approach; and an old hardwood strip floor gets the American country look with a whitewashed undercoat of translucent paint, followed by stenciled floral and butterfly motifs, all sealed with a clear finish.*

LEFT: *Faux patio bricks were stenciled on an interior cement floor; garden-style stepping stones can also be replicated in this way.*

ON THE SURFACE

Leaf, flower, fruit, and vegetable designs can lend the garden touch to walls in a host of creative ways.

CLOCKWISE, *from top left: A true work of art, this dramatic flowered "wallpaper" is hand painted with acrylics on canvas and then glued to the wall; decorative ceramic wall tiles with garden motifs can be introduced as accents on kitchen backsplashes, around doorways or windows, in a single row as a chair rail, or as part of a fireplace mantelpiece; and delicate leaves stamped in silver and blue paint float down a pale blue colorwashed wall.*

style tip

Choose one of the new wide wall-paper borders in a leaf, floral, or other nature motif to liven up walls and add a garden touch. Apply a border just beneath the crown molding or just above the wain-scoting or chair rail. Borders might also frame a window or even dress up a plain cabinet, wardrobe, or bookcase.

Textured wall surfaces add depth and a look of weathered antiquity to any room.

TOP, left to right: An old weathered door sal-vaged from the Italian countryside best displays its wonderful rough tex-ture and warm wood tones when propped casually against a wall; and decorative painting at its finest features hand-painted fruit tree branches over a textured background in a composition that pays homage to a famous set of ancient Roman wall frescoes known as "Empress Livia's Garden Room."

RIGHT: On a back-ground painted to resemble old stucco, the soft, faded color and graceful fruit-and-leaf motif of this border recall Italian fresco art.

THE SOFT TOUCH

MORE THAN ANY OTHER ELEMENTS, THE SOFT FURNISHINGS—RUGS, FABRICS, AND WOVEN FIBERS—LEND LIFE AND STYLE TO A ROOM. INTRODUCE COLOR, PATTERN, AND TEXTURE TO YOUR GARDEN ROOM WITH UPHOLSTERY, WINDOW TREATMENTS, LINENS, AND ACCESSORIES CHOSEN FOR THEIR FRESH, NATURE-LINKED LOOKS.

Table and bed linens that feature flowers, leaves, and insects are a natural choice for garden decorating.

TOP, *left to right:* Covering an ordinary patio dining set with a lively combination of grass green gingham and floral fabric is a fresh garden-style idea; and linen napkins silk-screened with blue flowers and butterflies bring the garden to the table.

CENTER, *left to right:* A feminine roses-and-lace atmosphere reigns in this bedroom lavishly furnished with mix-and-match linens that perfectly complement dainty white wicker; a cotton tablecloth features oversize flowers within an unusual vertical-striped border, all executed in fresh, light colors; and perky painted-wood dragonfly napkin rings are a charmingly unexpected table-setting detail.

LEFT: *Floral linen with an antique finish covers plump, inviting pillows, recalling the look of an English country house—the ultimate in traditional garden room style.*

113

THE SOFT TOUCH

Rugs and pillows are available in many delightful nature-inspired designs, both formal and informal.

CLOCKWISE, from top: Whimsical cotton rugs in cheery nature motifs are pure fun for baths, kitchens, children's rooms, or any space that could use a light garden touch; a sophisticated wool area rug features stylized floral borders in large- and small-scale patterns; and custom-made pillows marry awning-stripe cotton upholstery fabric with a floral design for a charming antique look.

Fabrics for all applications reflect the perennial popularity of garden motifs.

CLOCKWISE, *from top right: Floral-embroidered linens edged in crocheted lace soften a wood folding chair and lend it the look of Victorian luxury; an ottoman covered in a distinctive grapevine-motif fabric that contrasts with the neighboring chair's stripes draws the eye with its bold design; decorative throw pillows are a quick and easy vehicle for garden style, especially when covered in lush cut velvet, whose nap catches the light to reveal a subtle fern print; in a sophisticated take on the butterfly theme, this sun-colored pillow brings life and light to any room; leaf-print upholstery on a dining room chair makes a subtle reference to the garden; and silk upholstery and a roll pillow make a bold statement with strong colors and nature-linked patterns.*

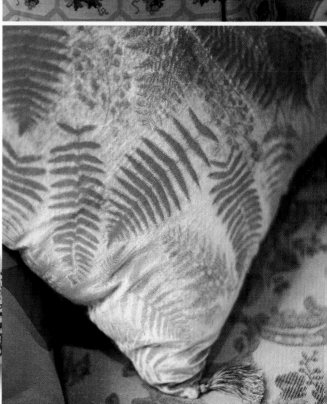

THE SOFT TOUCH

Window coverings—and the hardware that goes with them—are perfect vehicles for garden styling. These days finials and holdbacks (shown at top and bottom), as well as fabrics, can be found in many delightful garden motifs, from leaves to birds to pineapples.

ABOVE: Even tailored window treatments such as this Roman shade become garden friendly when executed in pretty, lightweight floral fabrics.

LEFT: A simple swag in a fresh floral fabric frames an attractive window while letting in light and views. Repeating the same fabric in other room elements unifies the look.

Curtains and shades reflecting many moods, from romantic to whimsical, add garden flair to windows.

TOP, *left and right:* Sheer panels in breezy prints and soft, subtle colors are the essence of an airy garden atmosphere; personal touches like a seashell dangling from a ribbon add to their charm. Such panels usually have their own loops or tabs for hanging on simple rods.

style tip

Add a little extra garden-style pizzazz to basic blinds made from natural materials such as reeds, grasses, rattan, and bamboo. Using a sewing machine or a hot glue gun, you can apply decorative accents or border trim in a garden-related design to the bottom of the blinds. Choose from the wide variety of fabric trim available at fabric and craft stores. For extra flair, add tassels at the blinds' top corners.

FURNISHINGS WITH FLAIR

YOU CAN BRING GARDEN STYLE INTO A ROOM WITH CHAIRS, TABLES, AND OTHER PIECES—OLD OR NEW—MEANT FOR THE PORCH OR PATIO. BUT EVEN TRADITIONAL INDOOR FURNITURE GAINS THAT FRESH-AIR FEELING WHEN IT'S UPHOLSTERED OR PAINTED IN GARDEN-INSPIRED COLORS AND PATTERNS.

Furniture made of twigs or wicker and other woven fibers has long been the choice for gardens and patios; now it's the perfect thing for indoor garden rooms, too.

CLOCKWISE, *from top left:* A porch and garden room classic since Victorian times, wicker gains fresh appeal when brightened with paint; rustic twig furniture is equally at home outdoors and indoors where, as here, cushions of French country–style fabric give it a certain sophistication (note the weathered shutter used as a decorative screen); a painted rattan chair and wheeled serving cart are jaunty partners on a porch; natural wicker is always a good choice for garden rooms and porches but must be protected from the elements if it is to be long-lived, just as cushions used outdoors must be covered in weather-resistant outdoor fabric; and painted wicker guarantees garden room ambience when it's mixed with pieces upholstered in floral fabrics.

FURNISHINGS WITH FLAIR

RIGHT: *Intricate mosaic tabletops fashioned from small pieces of stone, glass, or glazed ceramic tile, like this example from Morocco, are works of art as well as durable garden-style surfaces for eating and serving. Such tables usually have an iron base.*

BOTTOM RIGHT: *This elegant bamboo cabinet from the Philippines makes a dramatic focal point in a nature-inspired dining area; in addition, it offers practical storage for linens and tableware.*

style tip

Make an easy garden-style end table in a jiffy. Just select a large pot or urn, a birdbath, a cement garden pedestal, or any other fairly heavy, flat-topped garden ornament that's about the right height for an occasional table. Then top it with a proportional piece of heavy glass, round or square. Such tops can be purchased ready-made or cut to order at glass shops. For a larger coffee table, position a rectangular piece of glass across a matching pair of lower pedestals or pots.

CLOCKWISE, *from top left: An ornate reproduction Victorian birdcage becomes a garden-style table when topped with a piece of glass (it could easily hold a potted plant for an extra decorative touch; see page 132); this painted wood Adirondack-style table conjures up images of afternoons at the lake; painting stylized floral and leaf motifs on furniture is an old tradition in Europe, as well as a feature of American country decor; and details like these bent-bamboo door handles add a hint of the outdoors.*

OPPOSITE PAGE, CLOCKWISE *from top left: Outdoor furniture that could easily move indoors includes this highly original bench, whose back replicates a village of birdhouses (the motif reappears on the matching table); metal French bistro table and chairs that are good-looking indoors and make perfect guest seating for parties; this one-of-a-kind cast-iron bench, which would make a dramatic statement in a conservatory or sunroom; a comfortable Shaker-style porch rocker, a classic that has stood the test of time both indoors and out; and a contemporary wicker chair, painted in a fresh new color.*

THIS PAGE, CLOCKWISE *from top: A selection of contemporary garden chairs that look great in a room includes park bench–style seating with a little extra pizzazz in color and form (the back resembles the curved rise of a rocking chair); a sleek design in painted metal with a built-in perch for a drink; a sophisticated metal chair reminiscent of the wirework tradition in garden furniture; an original designer chair of tinted polymer composite; and a witty knockoff of a French bistro chair, whose cutout message echoes its sunny color.*

All of these are new chairs, but old ones can also take on new life when brought indoors. Old wicker, wood, or metal can be enjoyed in its distressed state after being cleaned and sprayed with a clear matte finish to prevent further deterioration. Rusted metal can be scrubbed with a wire brush and then rubbed with boiled linseed oil from the hardware store. The same oil also benefits old painted furniture. Of course, older pieces can also be stripped and painted in fresh contemporary colors for an entirely new look.

IN FROM THE GARDEN

ONE OF TODAY'S FRESHEST DECORATING IDEAS IS BRINGING GARDEN ARTIFACTS AND ORNAMENTS—NEW PIECES, ANTIQUES, AND FLEA MARKET FINDS—INDOORS. YOU CAN IMPORT EVERYTHING FROM WIRE BASKETS TO GARDEN GATES, FINIALS, AND SHUTTERS. HOW YOU USE AND DISPLAY THEM IS LIMITED ONLY BY YOUR IMAGINATION.

CLOCKWISE, *from top left: A decorative piece modeled on an antique birdcage makes a strong sculptural statement when placed on a tabletop or mantelpiece; a bamboo footwiper becomes a showstopper when placed, Japanese style, atop a table as a backdrop for a centerpiece; a cloche, or glass bell, used by gardeners to protect tender young seedlings makes a lovely see-through cover for fruit, cheese, or other delicacies on a buffet; a section of a 100-year-old iron garden gate has been furnished with a series of holders for old sap buckets sporting sprays of pepper berries—now the piece is a handsome objet d'art to be hung on a wall; cement finials replicate the stone ornaments found atop posts and walls of old buildings; gleaming ceramic fountain elements in hues of earth and sky reflect light in their water-slicked surfaces; and a lantern meant for the patio lends garden ambience and soft candlelight to an indoor scene when suspended from an iron hook on the wall.*

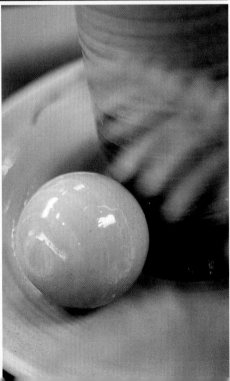

THIS PAGE, CLOCKWISE *from top left: A Zen aesthetic inspired this organic composition of recycled cinderblock embellished with carefully selected natural stones; an antique metal garden urn with its original base, all left in intriguingly weathered condition, makes a striking container for ivy; a section of old-fashioned cottage-style fencing, complete with post, becomes a room divider; an armillary-sphere sundial's strong lines and form show off to advantage atop a pedestal; and a large, glazed ceramic garden pot is a stylish holder for fireplace tools.*

OPPOSITE PAGE, CLOCKWISE *from bottom right: A study in earthly elements combines a cast-concrete pedestal table, stone spheres, a weathered figurine, and a terra-cotta pot; old garden fencing has a beautifully ornate form that looks striking against a white or solid-color wall; and a section of painted trellis brought indoors and propped against a wall makes an appealing garden-style accent above a desk, providing a handy place to tuck decorative cards as well as notes, reminders, and photos.*

IN FROM THE GARDEN

style tip

A vintage wood toolbox makes a great magazine rack. You can place it either on the floor or up on a narrow wood bench where the magazines will be easy to see. For a different twist, hang a toolbox on its side on the wall by nailing through the bottom and into the studs. With its handle facing out, parallel to the floor or countertop–voilà!–you have a towel rack.

LEFT: *This painted metal pot on its stand makes a delightful crayon holder (it could also hold pens and pencils or, at a buffet, eating utensils).*

RIGHT: *Terra-cotta ornaments meant for the garden can make wonderful lamp bases; they must be carefully drilled with a masonry bit to accommodate lamp hardware and cords.*

BELOW: *An antique European goat cart cradles extra bathroom towels (left), while a beautifully detailed clay flowerpot makes a handy home for kitchen utensils (right).*

ABOVE: *Many garden ornaments and accessories have sculptural shapes that can lend drama to a room. An oversize metal urn (left), holding a simple mounded planting of moss, draws all eyes in a living-room setting; a freestanding decorative garden obelisk (right) lends stature to a corner grouping of architectural pots.*

RIGHT: *Even a simple outdoor bench can be a charming indoor piece, either as a resting place for decorative accents or as a practical step stool or footrest.*

GREEN & GROWING

NOTHING SAYS "GARDEN" IN A ROOM QUITE LIKE BEAUTIFUL HEALTHY PLANTS. FLOWERS AND FOLIAGE INTRODUCE INSTANT FRESHNESS AND LIFE, AND YOU CAN ADAPT THEM TO SUIT ANY SPACE. MAKE A STATEMENT WITH ONE DRAMATIC PLANT, FILL A CORNER WITH A CONTAINER GARDEN, OR ARRANGE MINIATURE TOPIARIES ON A WINDOWSILL.

Plants and their containers are integral decorating elements in any garden room.

CLOCKWISE, from top left: Various examples of how simple pot and plant shapes become living sculptures include two dark ceramic bowls containing simple offerings of river stones and greenery; a matched pair of white ceramic containers and foliage plants; a bowl-size water garden featuring plantings of contrasting heights and textures; a bright bromeliad spotlighted in a pretty cachepot; an oxalis-filled dish with a cup as companion piece; and the strong sculptural shape of an agave plant.

GREEN & GROWING

style tip

Give a contemporary or timeworn bird-cage new life as a planter. (A cage with a removable bottom is easiest to work with.) Old cages should be cleaned and then primed, spray-painted, and sealed. You may wish to remove feeders, perches, and other accessories. Insert one or more plants in water-proof saucers and, if you like, line the cage's lower sides and corners with dampened sphagnum moss. You can easily reach plants with a small watering can that has a long, narrow spout.

ABOVE: *You can use exotic plants as ornaments to turn a quiet corner into an arresting scene like this one, which features a ponytail palm and small tillandsias. The accompanying pottery pieces and the painting behind them extend the sense of connection with traditional, earth-rooted cultures.*

LEFT: *A ceramic seashell, also filled with several varieties of tillandsia, is just the right scale for decorating a bathroom counter. Plant and container are carefully matched for their colors, tropical associations, and sculptural qualities.*

LEFT, *top and bottom: Formal garden style is easily introduced to a room through the use of appropriate plants and containers. A tall, weathered urn in the classical style, bearing a clipped evergreen, bespeaks 18th-century grandeur; and twin ivy topiaries in the distinguished company of small statuary and an antique clock exude old-world elegance.*

BELOW: *A more casual offering marries the charms of water and plants in a small "garden" within a clamshell bowl. Complete with a prized seashell and glass baubles reminiscent of fishermen's floats, it suggests a seaside retreat.*

133

DETAIL ORIENTED

WHEN IT COMES TO ADDING THE GARDEN TOUCH TO YOUR HOME, ALMOST ANYTHING WITH AN OUTDOOR OR NATURE THEME IS FAIR GAME. FROM BOTANICAL PRINTS TO TABLETOP FOUNTAINS, FROM ARTFUL ARRANGEMENTS OF STONES TO LEAF-PRINT LAMPSHADES, SPECIAL ACCENTS GIVE YOUR ROOM GARDEN-STYLE FLAIR.

TOP, *left to right:* Metal "leaves" add a nicely tailored touch to table napkins; bundled twigs form the base of a petite table lamp; and votives dangling in the glass holders of a wrought-iron chandelier bring soft light to an evening garden room scene.

CENTER, *left to right:* Fish and nets combine in a lively nature motif on a copper mirror frame from Pakistan; with their bright, painted-tin bodies and bottle-cap eyes, these blackbirds contribute humor to the nature theme; art and nature coexist with living callas in the foreground, painted fruit in the background; and a ceramic rooster struts his stuff on the wall.

LEFT: *Flowers and candles afloat in a glass bowl introduce grace notes of softness and romance to garden rooms.*

135

DETAIL ORIENTED

CLOCKWISE, *from top left: Handmade paper incorporating plant and leaf fragments was molded around a wire frame and suspended on a twig stem to make this delicate nature-inspired lamp; Wardian cases were popular display containers for indoor plants in Victorian times, and today's reproductions retain all the charm of miniature glasshouses; a mirror wreathed in a leafy metalwork garland and vases of hollowed stone combine to bring touches of the natural world to a mantelpiece; and a simple steel cone flower container is an appealing work of art in its own right.*

CLOCKWISE, *from top left: Candlelight and shimmering water never fail to evoke images of evenings spent outdoors in the garden; pressed fern leaves make a handsome pair of "portraits" within distressed wood reminiscent of old cottage window frames; a still life built around a small collection of sun-whitened ocean denizens embodies the spare beauty of the seashore; and elements of nature—wood, stone, and clay—can be brought together simply, with found objects, to remind the viewer of special moments spent outdoors.*

style tip

Be on the lookout for pretty garden-style objects, old and new, that you can use in original ways. This picket-fence box was intended to be a planter surround, but it makes a perfect holder for stationery and might inspire a similar look for your entire desk area.

DETAIL ORIENTED

RIGHT: *Running water is a particularly effective vehicle for bringing nature indoors—here, its audiovisual delights are exhibited in fountains of formal geometric shape (above) and the organic shapes of rocks (below).*

BOTTOM LEFT: *A colorful ceramic bowl of original design celebrates the abundance of the garden.*

OPPOSITE PAGE, *clockwise from top left: Cleverly painted and "cracked" to resemble a fragment of an old fresco, this garden scene's lovely soft color graces a wall over a fireplace; a mirror frame of a molded fiberglass-and-gypsum compound sports a lifelike relief of branching leaves, complemented by sculpted clay vases finished in gleaming copper and platinum; decorative fruit-patterned tiles escape the kitchen to go anywhere in the house; and botanical prints (like these, cut from wallpaper) are instant garden-style decorating elements that can be framed, decoupaged, or simply attached to surfaces using wallpaper glue.*

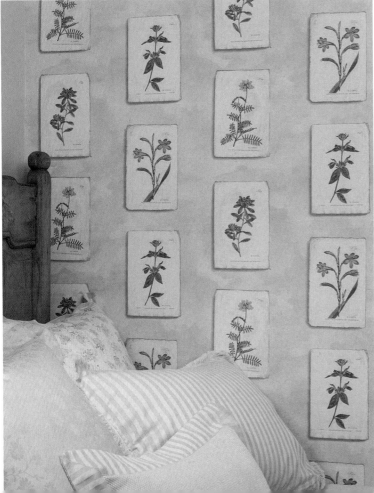

RESOURCES

Shopping for wall and floor coverings, furnishings, and accessories for garden rooms takes you on a delightful treasure hunt from salvage yards to garden-supply stores, antique marts, purveyors of fine furniture, and now the World Wide Web. The following is just a sampling of stores, manufacturers, and mail-order sources for garden-style decorating elements.

EAST

Campo de' Fiori
Route 7
Sheffield, MA 01257
413/528-9180
www.campodefiori.com
Indoor and outdoor furniture and accessories; handcrafted Mexican copper, bronze, and stone garden pieces

Gray Gardens Antiques
461 Broome Street
New York, NY 10013
212/966-7116
Vintage furnishings, architectural fragments, ornaments, and accessories

Marston Luce
1314 21st Street NW
Washington, DC 20036
202/775-9460
18th- and 19th-century French and Continental furniture, garden ornaments and accessories, architectural fragments; plants and topiaries

Mecox Gardens
257 County Road 39A
Southampton, NY 11968
631/287-5015 (also in East Hampton, NY, 516/329-9405; and New York, NY, 212/249-5301)
www.mecoxgardens.com
New and antique furniture, dishes, pots, plants, and minimalist accessories

Takashimaya
693 Fifth Avenue
New York, NY 10022
800/753-2038
New and antique furnishings, accessories, and ornaments

Michael D. Trapp
7 River Road
West Cornwall, CT 06796
860/672-6098
Garden antiques, furniture, and ornaments

Treillage Ltd.
418 East 75th Street
New York, NY 10021
212/535-2288
European-inspired ornaments, furniture, architectural pieces, and antiques

SOUTH

Charleston Gardens®
61 Queen Street
Charleston, SC 29401
843/723-0252 or 800/469-0118
www.charlestongardens.com
French and English furnishings, accessories, and gifts

The Elegant Earth
2901 2nd Avenue South
Birmingham, AL 35223
205/251-4695
American garden antiques and accessories; new European pots with an antique look

Florida Victorian Architectural Antiques and Salvage
112 West Georgia Avenue
Deland, FL 32720
904/734-9300
www.floridavictorian.com
Architectural fragments, ornaments, doors and windows, and garden statuary

Ryan Gainey and Company
2973 Hardman Court NE
Atlanta, GA 30305
404/233-2050
www.ryangainey.com
Garden ornaments and furniture; pieces by regional artisans and designers; iron pieces from Mexico

The Garden Trellis
8015 Maple Street
New Orleans, LA 70118
504/861-1953
Plants; new and vintage garden ornaments

MIDWEST

Antiquities and Oddities Architectural Salvage
2045 Broadway
Kansas City, MO 64108
816/283-3740
www.aoarchitecturalsalvage.com
Architectural fragments and ornaments

Camrose Hill Flower Studio and Farm
233 South Second Street
Stillwater, MN 55082
651/351-9631
New and vintage furniture and garden ornaments; dried and fresh flowers and topiaries; garden statuary

Casabella
5027 France Avenue South
Edina, MN 55410
952/927-4875
New and old furnishings, accessories, and architectural fragments; original decorative pieces from old found objects

Grandeur Gardens
223 West 47th Street
Kansas City, MO 64112
816/561-2212
www.grandeurgardens.com
Fountains, statues, urns, architectural pieces, accessories, and gifts

Jayson's Home & Garden
1911 North Clybourn Avenue (home)
1885 North Clybourn Avenue (garden)
Chicago, IL 60614
773/525-3100 (home)
773/248-8180 (garden)
Furniture, ornaments, and accessories; vintage tools; plants and containers

My Sister Shabby's Place on Fifth
304 Fifth Street
West Des Moines, IA 50265
888/742-2294
www.mysistershabbys.com
Furniture and accessories with an old-fashioned look

The Urban Gardener
1006 West Armitage Avenue
Chicago, IL 60614
773/477-2070 or 800/998-7330
www.urbangardenerchicago.com
Furniture, trellises, architectural fragments, pots, and weather-resistant fabrics

WEST

The Gardener
1836 Fourth Street
Berkeley, CA 94710
510/548-4545
and 516 Dry Creek Road
Healdsburg, CA 95448
707/431-1063
Furnishings and accessories for indoors and the garden, with a focus on natural materials and season-specific display

The Garden Gallery
3020 H Street
Sacramento, CA 95816
916/444-1844
Garden ornaments, accessories, fountains,
trellises, lighting, and furniture

GardenHome
1799 Fourth Street
Berkeley, CA 94710
510/559-7050
and 801 Main Street
St. Helena, CA 94574
707/967-4800
www.gardenhomeonline.com
Interior garden-style furnishings, linens,
dinnerware, accessories, gifts, and antique
architectural fragments

A Garden of Distinction
5819 Sixth Avenue South
Seattle, WA 98108
206/763-0517
www.agardenofdistinction.com
French garden antiques and accessories,
custom garden houses, stoneware pots, and
French tableware and linens

Great Jones Home
1921 Second Avenue
Seattle, WA 98101
206/448-9405
Vintage American and European furnishings,
linens, garden ornaments, and accessories

HerbanPottery
3220 First Avenue South
Seattle, WA 98134
206/621-8601
Garden ornaments, accessories, gifts, and
containers

In Any Event, Inc.
3036 Woodside Road
Woodside, CA 94062
650/851-3520
Interior and exterior accessories; linens,
dinnerware, and gifts; unusual containers
and pedestals; plants

Island Home
313 Marine Avenue
Balboa Island, CA 92662
949/673-1133
Garden ornaments, accessories, gifts, linens,
and furnishings

Ohmega Salvage
2400 and 2407 San Pablo Avenue
Berkeley, CA 94702
510/843-7368 and 510/204-0767
www.ohmegasalvage.com
Vintage architectural fragments; doors,
windows, fixtures, and hardware

Ohmega Too
2204 San Pablo Avenue
Berkeley, CA 94702
510/843-3636
www.ohmegatoo.com
Antique and reproduction lighting, plumb-
ing, doors, windows; garden ornaments

Pan's Garden
2360 Lillie Avenue
Summerland, CA 93067
www.pansgarden.net
805/969-6859
Furniture, fountains, ornaments, and
accessories; plants and pots

Pullman & Company
108 Throckmorton Avenue
Mill Valley, CA 94941
415/383-0847
Vintage American and European furnishings,
linens, garden ornaments, and accessories

Roger's Gardens
2301 San Joaquin Hills Road
Corona del Mar, CA 92625
949/640-5800
www.rogersgardens.com
Furnishings, ornaments, home accessories,
and gifts; plants and containers

The Sitting Room
Ginger Barber Designs
2402 Quenby Street
Houston, TX 77005
713/523-1932
www.thesittingroom.net
Room settings featuring vintage and new
garden-style furnishings and accessories,
dried topiaries, and pots

Stone Grove
164 Main Street
Los Altos, CA 94022
650/941-8777
and 670 Main Street
Pleasanton, CA 94566
925/484-3751
Garden ornaments, fountains, furnishings,
and accessories

Treillage Ltd.
135 Post Street (in Gump's)
San Francisco, CA 94108
415/982-1616
www.gumps.com
Garden ornaments, furniture, architectural
pieces, containers, and books; new and
antique garden lighting

Wickets Garden Antiques
8823 Beverly Boulevard
Los Angeles, CA 90048
800/585-1225
European indoor and outdoor furniture and
garden ornaments; antique tools

Wisteria/Aptos Gardens
5870 Soquel Drive
Soquel, California 95073
831/462-2900 (Wisteria)
831/462-3859 (Aptos Gardens)
New and antique furniture, accessories,
garden ornaments, dinnerware, linens; plants

Yard Art
2188 1/2 Sutter Street
San Francisco, CA 94115
415/346-6002
www.yardartsf.com
Antique and weathered garden objects;
architectural salvage and fragments

MANUFACTURERS

Amdega-Machin Conservatories
800/449-7348
www.amdega.com
or www.machin-conservatories.com

British Conservatories
800/566-6360
www.britishrose.com

Brunschwig & Fils
212/838-7878
www.brunschwig.com
Fine fabrics

Four Seasons Sunrooms & Conservatories
800/368-7732
www.fourseasonsunrooms.com

French Wyres
P. O. Box 131655
Tyler, TX 75713
903/561-1742
www.frenchwyres.com
American-made wire garden furnishings

Hunter Douglas
800/937-7895
http://209.170.18.141/index.html
Blinds, shades, and other window treatments

Oak Leaf Conservatories
800/360-6283
www.traditional-building.com/brochure/
oakleaf.html

L. & J. G. Stickley, Inc.
Stickley Drive, P. O. Box 480
Manilus, NY 13104-0480
315/682-5500
www.stickley.com
Garden-style furniture

Waverly
800/423-5881
www.waverly.com
Coordinated fabrics and wallpapers

MAIL ORDER/CATALOGS
(call for retail store locations)

Crate & Barrel
800/323-5461
www.crateandbarrel.com

Delaware River Trading Company
800/732-4791
www.delawarerivertrading.com

Fran's Wicker & Rattan Furniture
800/531-1511
www.franswicker.com

Gardener's Eden
800/822-1214 (customer service)
800/822-9600 (orders)

Pottery Barn
800/922-9934 (customer service)
800/922-5507 (orders)
www.potterybarn.com

Smith & Hawken
800/776-3336
www.smithandhawken.com

Wicker Warehouse
800/989-4253
www.wickerwarehouse.com

DESIGN and PHOTOGRAPHY CREDITS

DESIGN

FRONT MATTER

1 Designer: Elizabeth Kirkpatrick

GARDEN ROOM STYLE

6-7 Interior Designer: Hilary Thatz; Builder/Architect: Dennis J. O'Connor, Design/Build; Garden Designer: Marilee A. Gaffney 10-11 top Interior Designer: Paulette Trainor 12 top Interior Designer: J. Reed Robbins 13 top Interior Designer: Carol S. Shawn 15 Interior Designer: Peg Van Dyne 17 Architect: Rob Whitten 18 top Garden Designer: Keeyla Meadows 21 Interior Designer: Susan Federman and Maria Johnston 22 Designer: Robert Bellamy; Stylist: Mary Jane Ryburn 23 top Interior Designer: Trish Dietze 24 top right Floral Designer: Charlie Thigpen 24 bottom Architect: Tucker & Marks, Inc. 25 Interior Designer: Linda Applewhite 26 top Designer: Steve Chase 27 Interior Designer: John D. Oetgen 29 top Designers: Teresa and Tyler Beard 29 bottom Interior Designers: Kay and Jimmy Fuller; Architect: Neil Turner 32 top Designers: Ginger Langford and Randi Herman/GardenHome 32 bottom Interior Designers: Sanborn Design, Inc., and Molly Agras 33 Architect: Backen, Arragoni & Ross 34 top Tile: Buddy Rhodes Studio/Amalfi Tile & Marble; Designer: Minor Revisions Architecture & Design; Contractor: Mark McCarthy 34 bottom Interior Designer: Julie Atwood Design & Restoration; Window Treatment: Lun-On Company 36 top Decorative Painter: James Hartman 37 top Designer: Elizabeth Kirkpatrick

BEAUTIFUL ROOMS

38-39 Interior Designer: Mel Lowrance 40-41 Interior Designer: Kit Parmentier/Allison Rose 44-45 Interior Designer: Susan Federman/ Federman, Johnston 46-47 Stylist: Charles Reiley 48 Designer: Elizabeth Kirkpatrick 49 top right Designer: Loretta Gargan Landscape + Design 49 middle right Decorative Painter: James Hartman 49 bottom left Designer: Jenny Venegas 49 bottom right The Gardener 50-51 Architect: Jarvis Architects 54-55 Interior Designer: Linda Applewhite 56 top left Designers: Ginger Langford and Randi Herman/GardenHome 56 top right Interior Designer: Monty Collins

and Willem Racké 57 Designer and Decorative Painter: Peggy del Rosario 58-59 Interior Designer: Alison Lufkin/Sullivan & Company 60-61 Interior Designer: Susan Hunter; Architect: Daniel Hunter; Landscape Architect: Ralph Alexander & Associates; Builder: Bertotti Landscaping Inc. 62 Interior Designer: Trish Dietze; Floral Stylist: Tom Stokey 63 top left and right Designer and Decorative Painter: Peggy del Rosario 64-65 top center and 64 bottom right Designers: Ginger Langford and Randi Herman/GardenHome 64 bottom left The Gardener 65 bottom left Design: Peter O. Whiteley 65 bottom right Interior Designer: FJ Interior Design; Floral Arrangements: Gayle Nicoletti/Bloomin Gayles 67 top Homestead 67 middle left and right Interior Designers: Camille Fanucci/ Interior Design Concepts and Patricia Whitt Designs 68-69 Interior Designer: Kathryne Dahlman/Kathryne Designs 70 top left The Gardener 71 Decorative Painting: The Beardsley Company 72-73 Designer: Loretta Gargan Landscape + Design 74 bottom and 75 Decorative Painter: Shelley Masters 76 top left Designer: Loretta Gargan Landscape + Design 76 top right Design: Tsetse/The Gardener 76 bottom Orchard Nursery "Lazy K" House 77 top left Design: Great Jones Home; Floral Design: Fleurish 77 bottom left and right The Gardener 78-79 Architect: Richard Schadt/ Richard Schadt Associates, Inc. 80 Decorative Painter: Samantha Renko Decorative Arts Studio 81 top right Interior Designer: Osborn Design; Decorative Painter: Iris Potter 81 bottom left Decorative Painter: Samantha Renko Decorative Arts Studio

LIVING INSIDE OUT

84 Designers: Sarah and Walter Brown 85 Designers: Jim Zirkel and Michael Sopoliga/Home Design Services, Inc.; Interior Designer: Sharon M. Gilkey 86-87 Interior Designers: Michaela Scherer Interior Design and RozaLynn Woods Interior Design 88-89 Designer: Rosmari Agostini; Stylist: Mary Jane Ryburn 90-91 Designers: Jenny and Peter Venegas 92-93 Designers: Sarah Jernigan and Ellen Riley 96 Designer: Marc Whitman, Whitman Architectural Design 97 top Landscape Architect: The Berger Partnership 97 bottom Designer: Steve Chase 98-99 Architect: Backen,

Arragoni & Ross 101 top and bottom Design: Karen Taddei/Lilacs 102-103 Interior Designer: Melissa Griggs; Architect/Builder: Bill Galli; Decorative Painter: Adele Crawford; Landscape Designer: Peter Koenig 104-105 Interior Designer: Claudia Fleury/ Claudia's Designs

ELEMENTS OF STYLE

107 GardenHome 108 Decorative Painter: Shelley Masters 109 top left Architect: Remick Associates Architects-Builders, Inc.; Tile: Stonelight Tiles 109 top center The Gardener 109 top right Design: Taylor Woodrow 109 middle left Design: Country Floors/Native Tile & Ceramics 109 center Roger's Gardens 109 center right Design: Laura Taylor Moore/ Interior Services of Los Gatos and Betty Benesi/Cottage Industries; Stencil: Jonathan Davis 110 left Decorative Painting: The Beardsley Company 110 top right, clockwise from left Tile Visions; Diane Swift; Fireclay Tile 110 bottom Decorative Painter: Justina Jorrin Barnard 111 top left Designer: Elizabeth Kirkpatrick 111 top right Decorative Painter: Shelley Masters 111 bottom left Wallpaper: Waverly 112 Interior Designer: Linda Knight Carr 113 top left Stylist: Julie Atwood 113 middle center Interior Designer: Alison Lufkin/Sullivan & Company 113 bottom left Sarah Kaplan/Great Jones Home 114 bottom left Interior Designer: Kit Parmentier/ Allison Rose 115 top left and middle left GardenHome 115 middle right Interior Designer: Richard Witzel & Associates 115 bottom right GardenHome 116 top left Design: Rue de France, www.ruedefrance@ efortress.com 116 top right Interior Designers: Karen Davis and Cañada College Student ASID; Window Treatment: Marti M. Woo 117 top left Interior Designer: Kit Parmentier/ Allison Rose 117 top right Design: Elizabeth Kirkpatrick 117 bottom Design: Lynne Barry Roe 118 GardenHome 120 top and bottom right The Gardener 121 top left and bottom right GardenHome 121 top right Design: Stephen Kanner/Kanner Architects 121 bottom left The Gardener 122 top left Eric Cortina/ Roger's Gardens 123 top Sheila Noyes/Island Home 123 bottom left Designer: Mario Bellini/The Gardener 123 bottom right Chair Design: Tivoli; Architect: Sam Wells & Associates;

Stylist: Julie Atwood **124** Designer: Elizabeth Kirkpatrick **125 top left and bottom right** Eric Cortina/ Roger's Gardens **125 top center and right, and bottom left** The Gardener **125 middle right** GardenHome **125 bottom center** Designer: Stefan Prochaska/The Gardener **126 top left** Designer: Loretta Gargan Landscape + Design **126 top right** GardenHome **127 top right** Designer: Elizabeth Kirkpatrick **127 bottom left** GardenHome **128 top right** Designer: Elizabeth Kirkpatrick **128 bottom left** Interior Designer: Claudia Fleury/ Claudia's Designs **129 top left** Interior Designer: Kaidan Erwin/Tucker & Marks, Inc. **129 top right** Eric Cortina/Roger's Gardens **130** Interior Designer: Thomas Bartlett Interiors of Napa **131 top left and right, middle right, and bottom left** Designer: Loretta Gargan Landscape + Design **131 middle left** Interior Designers: Michaela Scherer Interior Design and RozaLynn Woods Interior Design **131 bottom right** Eric Cortina/Roger's Gardens **132 bottom left** Design: Davis Dolbok/Living Room **133 top left** Interior Designer: Bill Key **133 right** Designer: Wilson Murray Design **135 top left and center, middle right, and bottom left** GardenHome **135 top right and middle left** The Gardener **135 middle, second from left** Artist: Tracy Fitzgerald/The Gardener **135 middle, second from right** Artist: Mei-Yu Lo/The Gardener **136 top left** Interior Designer: Jeanease Rowell Design **136 top right** Eric Cortina/ Roger's Gardens **136 bottom left and right** The Gardener **137 top left** GardenHome **137 top right** Eric Cortina/Roger's Gardens **137 middle and bottom right** Designer: Loretta Gargan Landscape + Design **138 top** GardenHome **138 bottom right** Design: Sespe Fountain/The Gardener **138 bottom left** Artist: Susan Hall/The Gardener **139 top right** Artists: Rosaria Rattin (ceramics) and Deborah Childress (mirror)/The Gardener **139 bottom left** "Idea house" at San Francisco Design Center **139 bottom right** Vietri

BACK MATTER

140 and 144 Eric Cortina/Roger's Gardens

PHOTOGRAPHY

Unless otherwise credited, all photographs are by **Philip Harvey.**

Jean Allsopp: 24 top right, 112; **Noel Barnhurst:** 65 bottom left; **Antoine Bootz:** 27, 84-85 center; **Van Chaplin:** 16 left, 132 top right, 133 bottom; **Peter Christiansen:** 26 top, 97 bottom, 122 bottom right; **Tina Cornett:** 92-93 all; **Mark Darley/ESTO:** 24 bottom; **Ken Druse:** 16 top, 18 top, 36 bottom, 49 top left, 65 top right, 100, 101 middle right; **Derek Fell:** 8 middle; **Tria Giovan:** 10 bottom, 35 both, 37 bottom, 46 all, 47, 49 middle left, 56 bottom right, 95 bottom, 119 top left, middle right, and bottom right, 123 middle right; **Ken Gutmaker:** 2 left, 6-7, 25, 50-51 all, 54-55 all, 58 top left and bottom, 59, 60-61 all, 65 bottom right, 102-103 all, 104-105 all, 113 center, 126 bottom left and right, 128 bottom left; **Jamie Hadley:** 1, 23 top, 31, 37 top, 40 top left and bottom right, 41, 48, 62 top, 67 middle and right, 68 top left, 68-69 center, 69 top and bottom, 78-79 all, 87 top and middle, 108, 111 top left and right, 114 bottom left and right, 116 middle left, 117 top left and right, 120 left, 123 top, 124, 127 top right and left, 128 top and bottom right, 131 middle left, 132 bottom, 139 bottom right; **Lynne Harrison:** 19 top; **Jenifer Jordan:** 14 middle and bottom, 15, 29 top, 67 top, 70 bottom, 109 bottom left; **Barry Lewis:** 22, 88 both, 89 bottom, 115 top right; **David Duncan Livingston:** 8 top and bottom, 9, 12 bottom, 28 bottom, 30 both, 63 bottom, 81 top left, 85 bottom, 111 bottom right, 119 top right, 127 bottom right, 139 top; **Peter Malinkowski/In Site:** 96; **Sylvia Martin:** 85 top, 133 top left; **Steven Mays:** 110 bottom right;

E. Andrew McKinney: 10-11 center, 21, 38-39, 44, 45 top right and bottom left, 49 bottom left, 56 top right, 74 all, 75 top, 80, 81 bottom left, 82-83, 90-91 all, 111 bottom left, 113 top right and middle right, 114 top left and right, 115 bottom left and middle right, 116 top and bottom, 117 bottom, 122 top left, 125 top left and bottom right, 128 top left, 129 all, 131 bottom right, 132 top left, 133 right, 136 top left and right, 137 top right and bottom left, 139 bottom left, 140, 144; **Emily Minton:** 29 bottom, 94 top left; **Bradley Olman:** 134; **Gary W. Parker:** 98 bottom; **David Phelps:** 86-87 center, 87 bottom; **Norman A. Plate:** 121 top right; **Richard Rethemeyer:** 122 middle right; **Tom Rider:** 113 top left, 123 bottom right; **Eric Roth:** 77 top right, 94 bottom left, 101 top and bottom; **Sibila Savage:** 2 right, 5 and 6 border, 20 middle, 23 middle, 24 top left, 38 border, 40 bottom left, 45 top left, 49 top right, 53 bottom right, 58 top right, 62 bottom, 67 bottom left, 68 top right, 72-73 all, 75 bottom, 76 top left, 82 border, 84 bottom, 89 top, 95 top, 97 top left, 99 top and bottom right, 106 border, 109 bottom right, 113 bottom right, 119 middle left, 125 middle left, 126 top left, 131 top left and right, middle right, center, and bottom left, 135 bottom right, 137 middle and bottom right; **Chris Shorten:** 122 bottom left; **Michael Skott:** 4, 11 bottom, 14 top, 16 bottom, 19 bottom, 20 top and bottom, 42-43 all, 52, 53 top, 66, 77 top left, 94 middle, 113 middle left and bottom left, 119 bottom left, 126 middle right, 143; **Ron Sutherland:** 81 bottom right; **Michael S. Thompson:** 26 middle and bottom, 28 top; **Brian Vanden Brink:** 17; **Dominique Vorillon:** 70 top right; **David Wakely:** 36 top, 49 middle right

INDEX

Architectural fragments, decorating with, 54-55, 60-61, 75, 90, 111, 119
Asian style, 28, 70, 72-73, 74-75, 86-87
Bathrooms, 12, 20, 70-71, 132
Bedrooms, 21, 36, 66-67, 113, 124, 143
Birdcages as decor, 81, 102, 121, 125, 130, 132
Birdhouses as decor, 11, 15, 36, 42-43, 49, 52, 90, 122
Candlelight, 32-33, 56, 64-65, 125, 135, 137
Collections, displaying, 23, 36, 42-43, 48-49, 53, 90
Color, tips for using, 20-25, 57, 88
Conservatories
    examples of, 6-7, 44-45, 46-47, 58-59, 60-61, 78-79, 130
    history of, 8-9, 16
    miniature, 136
Containers
    for cut flowers, 12, 14, 49, 64-65, 72-73, 76-77, 103, 136, 139
    for living plants, 40, 46, 72-73, 74, 75, 86-87, 126, 129, 131-133
    new uses for garden, 23, 92-93, 120, 126, 128, 135
Contemporary style, 10-11, 28, 30, 63, 72-73, 94, 97
Country style
    American, 11, 36-37, 42-43, 49, 81, 90-91, 94, 95, 122, 123
    European, 24, 54-55, 57, 62, 80-81, 102-103, 104-105
Decorating ideas, sources of, 18-19, 23. See also Resources
Design principles, 20-29
Dining areas
    fresh-air, 22, 60, 85, 98-99, 104, 113
    indoor, 8, 11, 13, 30, 33, 47, 59, 62-63, 75
Entertaining, ideas for, 64-65, 92-93
Fabrics
    decorating with, 26, 41, 68-69, 88, 105, 112-117
    protecting, 119
Faux effects, 23, 36, 69, 80-81, 105, 109
Floor coverings, 51, 52, 86-87, 114
Flooring, 108-109
    stone, 10-11, 40-41, 51, 68-69, 74-75, 98-99, 102-103
    tile, 26, 34, 109
    wood, 21, 109
Flowers
    displaying, 14, 42-43, 76-77, 89, 136
    as inspiration, 18-19, 23, 26, 52-53, 71, 110
    spaces for arranging, 31, 100-101
Folk art, 42-43, 62
Fountains. See Water features
Furniture, 86-87, 96-97, 118-123
    outdoor, brought in, 11, 34-35, 37, 40-41, 122-123, 129
    protecting, 119, 123
Garden accessories
    indoors, 34, 37, 124-129
    new uses for, 35, 70, 92-93, 120, 125-128
Garden houses, 102-103
Home office spaces, 12, 32, 137
Kitchens, 25, 34, 56-57, 81, 104, 134

Lamps, 55, 128, 135, 136
Leaf motifs, 14, 26-27, 68-69, 115
Lighting, 24, 32-33, 98-99
Light, natural, 12, 24, 30-31, 50-51
Mediterranean style, 22, 25, 57, 81, 104-105
Mirrors, 27, 30, 53, 135, 136, 139
Natural elements, using, 10-11, 28, 34, 72-73, 94, 136
Nighttime effects, 32-33, 98-99
Offices. See Home office spaces
Paint, decorative, 36, 49, 57, 71, 74-75, 108, 110, 111, 119, 121, 143. See also Faux effects; Stenciling; Trompe l'oeil; Wall treatments
Patterns
    decorating with, 26-29, 40-41, 114-115
    scale of, 26-27, 29, 58
Plants, decorating with, 10-11, 37, 72-73, 74-75, 78-79, 130-133
Porches, 83, 86-87, 90-91, 94-95, 113, 118
Pots. See Containers
Resources, 140-141
Romantic style, 15, 20, 88-89, 113
Skylights, 6-7, 30, 44-45, 50-51
Small spaces, ideas for, 14, 58-59
Southwestern style, 29, 96

Stenciling, 14, 109
Style tips, 111, 117, 120, 127, 132, 137
Sunrooms, 10-11, 17, 26, 35, 37, 40-41
Tableaux, arranging, 10, 14, 37, 42, 45, 46, 49, 51, 55, 88, 137
Table-setting ideas, 64-65, 92-93, 113
Textures, decorating with, 28-29, 44-45, 63
Topiary, 10, 51, 56, 62, 66, 90-91, 133
Trellises indoors, 7, 15, 46, 127
Trompe l'oeil, 12, 23, 80-81, 105
Tropical style, 6-7, 10-11, 17, 44-45, 64, 68-69, 78-79
Urns. See Containers
Verandas, 84-85, 88-89, 96-97, 98-99
Victorian style, 8-9, 16, 19, 46, 60-61, 88-89, 97
Wall treatments, 36, 57, 71, 80-81, 108, 110-111
Water features, 78-79, 105, 125, 133, 138
Window treatments, 116-117
    blinds, 34, 68, 94, 117
    curtains and draperies, 21, 35, 68-69, 117
    screens, 94-95
    shades, 56, 86-87, 116
    swags, 57, 116
Winter retreats, 16-17